GRADE 2

FINISH LINE

Writing

for the Common Core State Standards

Continental

Acknowledgments

Illustrations: Page 54, 65, 71, 72: Ruth Flanigan; Page 160, 171 *chart and map:* Laurie Conley; Page 171 *butterfly diagram:* Estella Hickman; Page 196: Carol O'Malia

Photographs: Page 7: Ryan McVay; Page 24: www.istockphoto.com/kovalus; Page 30: www.istockphoto.com/bonniej; Page 35: ©Royalty-Free/Corbis; Page 83: Courtesy of Annick Press; Page 91: www.istockphoto.com/Griselda Amorim; Page 99: PhotoLink; Page 107: PhotoLink; Page 117: www.istockphoto.com/Patrick Robbins; Page 123: Getty Images Royalty Free; Page 133: C Squared Studios; Page 139: www.istockphoto.com/HTuller; Page 147: NASA-JPL; Page 164: Image used under GNU Licensing from Stefan Volk; Page 170: www.istockphoto.com/DanSchmitt

ISBN 978-0-8454-6765-7

Copyright © 2011 The Continental Press, Inc.

No part of this publication may be reproduced in any form or by any means, electronic, mechanical, photocopying, recording, or otherwise, without the prior written permission of the publisher. All rights reserved. Printed in the United States of America.

Table of Contents

Welcome to Finish Line Writing for the Common Core State Standards

This book will help you become a good writer. It will also help you get ready for writing tests.

The lessons in this book follow the Common Core State Standards for English Language Arts and Literacy in History, Social Studies, Science, and Technical Subjects. The Common Core State Standards (CCSS) build on the education standards developed by the states. This book will help you practice the writing skills you need.

In the lessons of this book, you will review the writing process. Then you will use those skills in different types of writing. You will also read informational text and stories. Then you will answer multiple-choice and writing questions about them. The lessons are in three parts:

- The first part talks about the writing skill you are going to study and explains what it is and how you use it.

- The second part is called Guided Practice. You will get more than practice here; you will get help. You will read a nonfiction passage and answer questions about it. After each question, the correct answer will be explained or a sample answer will be given. So you will answer questions and find out right away if you were correct.

- The third part is Test Yourself. Here you will read a question and then write an answer on your own.

After you have finished all of the lessons and units, you will take a Practice Test at the end of the book.

Now you are ready to begin using this book. Good luck!

© The Continental Press, Inc.   DUPLICATING THIS MATERIAL IS ILLEGAL.

Elements of Writing

You know what writing is. You know there are different kinds of writing. This unit tells about writing.

- **In Lesson 1,** you'll learn about the five steps in writing. You use these every time you write.

- **Lesson 2** tells about paragraphs. You will find out what makes a good paragraph.

- **Lesson 3** is about the main idea. It is also about the details. The details help explain the main idea.

- **Lesson 4** tells about cause and effect. This type of writing helps the reader know what happened. It also helps the reader know why it happened.

- **In Lesson 5,** you'll learn to write about how two things are alike. You'll also learn to write about how they are not alike.

© The Continental Press, Inc.   DUPLICATING THIS MATERIAL IS ILLEGAL.

The Writing Process

W.2.2, 3, 5, 6

Writing is a process. It takes a number of steps. Most writers follow these five steps:

Prewriting → Drafting → Revising → Editing → Publishing

Here is an easy way to remember the writing process. First, you **plan** what you will write. This step is prewriting. Next, you **write.** This step is drafting. Then you go back and **change** your writing. This step is revising. In the last step, you **check,** or edit, your work. This means you proofread. You fix mistakes in spelling and punctuation. Finally, you publish, or **show,** your writing.

Step 1: Prewriting

Think about these steps in this stage:

Read
Note
Organize

- Why are you writing? This is called your **purpose.**
- What will you write about? This is called your **subject.**
- What will you say? This is called your **content.**
- How will you say it? This is called your **voice.**
- Who will read it? This is called your **audience.**

© The Continental Press, Inc.   DUPLICATING THIS MATERIAL IS ILLEGAL.

Sometimes, you are writing for a test. Here is a test question that a student named Jameson answered. He read the question. Then he underlined important words.

Write a <u>story</u> about <u>learning to do something</u>. It could be about learning to play a game, ride a bike, or play the piano. Be sure to <u>tell how and why</u> you learned to do it. When writing your story, be sure to include:

- a title for your story
- a beginning, middle, and end to your story
- details to make your story interesting

The important words tell you what to do. The purpose is to tell how and why you learned to do something. The subject is learning to do something. You need to think about what you will write. Make notes about what you will write.

Read
Note
Organize

© The Continental Press, Inc.   DUPLICATING THIS MATERIAL IS ILLEGAL.

Sometimes, a graphic organizer can help you plan what you will write. This is like drawing a picture of your ideas. It can help you put your ideas in order. A story map is one type of a graphic organizer. Here is the story map Jameson used.

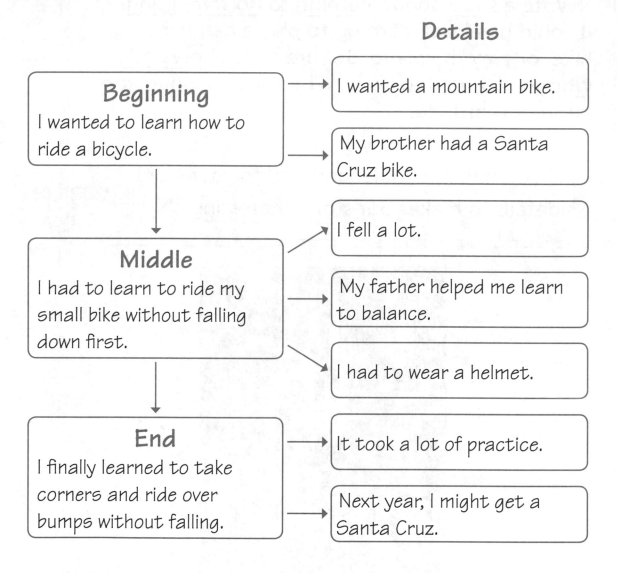

Details

Beginning
I wanted to learn how to ride a bicycle.

I wanted a mountain bike.

My brother had a Santa Cruz bike.

Middle
I had to learn to ride my small bike without falling down first.

I fell a lot.

My father helped me learn to balance.

I had to wear a helmet.

End
I finally learned to take corners and ride over bumps without falling.

It took a lot of practice.

Next year, I might get a Santa Cruz.

© The Continental Press, Inc.   DUPLICATING THIS MATERIAL IS ILLEGAL.

Guided Practice

Read the questions. Then answer them.

> The class must write a paper. The paper is about an important person. It must tell who the person is. It must give facts about why he or she is important. The paper is to be one page or two pages.

Who is the audience?

  A classmates

  B teacher

  C parents

  D principal

> The teacher has given the assignment. He is the audience. Choice B is the correct answer. Choices A, C, and D are incorrect. These people will not read the paper.

Which of these words would you underline to help understand the question?

  A important person

  B class

  C tell

  D must

> The paper is about an important person. This is the subject. Choice A is the correct answer. Choices B, C, and D are incorrect. They do not tell what to do.

© The Continental Press, Inc.   DUPLICATING THIS MATERIAL IS ILLEGAL.

Step 2: Drafting

You now have a plan. It is now time to write. This step is called **drafting.** A writer puts the ideas into sentences and paragraphs. Here is the draft Jameson wrote using his story map.

When I was 5, I wanted a bike to ride like my brother. He had a Santa cruz. It was a mountain bike. my bike was small. It had training wheels on it. All of my friends could ride there bikes. I did not no how to ride a real good bike. I asked my dad to teach me. He said I had to learn how to ride mine first. Before I could ride a mountain bike. It was hard to learn. I felt left out. I fell down a lot corners was hard. I fell once when I hit a rock. My dad he said he would help me balance. He held the bike and ran. I wore a helmet. It is for safety. I practiced a lot. It took a long time. and I finally learnd how. My dad he said maybe next year I can get a mountain bike.

Step 3: Revising

You are finished writing. Now, you read what you have written. Then you make changes to make your writing better. You change what you wrote. This is called **revising.** Ask yourself these questions. Your answers will help you think about changes you should make.

© The Continental Press, Inc.   DUPLICATING THIS MATERIAL IS ILLEGAL.

Content

- Does my writing have a main idea?
- Do I need to add any details?
- Do I need to take out details that aren't important?
- Does my writing have a beginning, middle, and end?

Structure

- Are my ideas clear?
- Are my sentences clearly written?

Guided Practice

Read Jameson's revised story. Look for changes. Then answer the questions.

When I was 5, I wanted a bike to ride like my brother.

He had a Santa cruz. ~~It was a~~ mountain bike. my bike was

small. ~~It~~ and had training wheels on it. All of my friends could

ride there bikes. I did not no how to ride a real good bike. I

asked my dad to teach me. He said I had to learn how to

ride mine first. ~~Before I could ride a mountain bike.~~ It was

hard to learn. (I felt left out.) I fell down a lot corners was

hard. I fell once when ^my bike^ I hit a rock. My dad he said he would

help me balance. He held the bike and ran ^alongside^. I wore a helmet.

~~It is~~ for safety. I practiced a lot. ~~It took a long time.~~ and I

finally learnd how. My dad he said maybe next year I can get

a mountain bike.

© The Continental Press, Inc.   DUPLICATING THIS MATERIAL IS ILLEGAL.

What sentence did Jameson move?

_____

_____

✓ **The proofreading marks tell you what changes were made. Here is the answer:**

I felt left out.

Why do you think he moved the sentence?

_____

_____

_____

✓ **The sentences should follow each other in a clear order. They should be with ideas that are alike. Here is a sample answer:**

Jameson moved it because it did not fit where it was. It fits better with the sentence about not being able to ride a bike like his friends.

© The Continental Press, Inc. DUPLICATING THIS MATERIAL IS ILLEGAL.

What details did Jameson add or take out?

_____

_____

_____

✓ Details should support the main idea. They should add information. They should be about the subject. Here is a sample answer:

Jameson added the words my bike and alongside. He took out the sentence "It took a long time." He also took out the phrase, "Before I could ride a mountain bike."

Write a title for the story.

_____

✓ The title sums up the main idea of an article or story. Here is a sample answer:

"How I Learned to Ride a Bike"

© The Continental Press, Inc.   DUPLICATING THIS MATERIAL IS ILLEGAL.

Peer Review

The teacher might sometimes have students work in pairs to edit each other's papers. This is called **peer editing** or **peer review.** Students use a checklist, or **rubric,** to do this. The checklist explains what is needed to receive a certain score on a writing paper.

The checklist tells what is expected for a range of scores. Sometimes, one checklist is used for the whole writing task. Other times, two checklists are used. One is for the content and how it is developed. The other is for grammar, punctuation, and capitalization. Checklists for writing may differ but they should look something like the one on page 15.

© The Continental Press, Inc.   DUPLICATING THIS MATERIAL IS ILLEGAL.

Checklist for Writing a Story

Score 3
- The writing answers all parts of the question.
- There is a clear beginning, middle, and end to the story.
- Details are interesting and are in a sensible order.
- The writing is easy to read and stays on the subject.
- Capitalization and punctuation are correct.

Score 2
- The writing answers almost all parts of the question.
- Parts of the beginning, middle, or end of the story are not clear.
- Not all details are in order or make sense.
- The writing mostly sticks to the subject, but some details don't belong.
- There are some mistakes in capitalization and punctuation.

Score 1
- The writing answers only part of the question.
- There is not a clear beginning, middle, or end to the story.
- Many details are missing or the order is unclear.
- The writing is off the subject in many places.
- There are many mistakes in capitalization and punctuation.

© The Continental Press, Inc.   DUPLICATING THIS MATERIAL IS ILLEGAL.

Step 4: Editing

Now, you are ready to edit. Look for mistakes in spelling, capitalization, and punctuation. You proofread to make sure that

- subjects and verbs go together
- punctuation marks are correct
- all words are spelled correctly
- proper nouns are capitalized

The chart below shows you some proofreading marks.

Proofreading Symbols	
∧ Add letters or words.	He had a bike. *mountain* ∧
⊙ Add a period.	I liked mountain bikes, too⊙
≡ Capitalize a letter.	≡it was small.
⩘ Add a comma.	When I was 5⩘ I wanted to ride a bike.
ℐ Delete letters or words.	My dad ~~he~~ said he would teach me.
∿ Switch the position of letters or words.	I learned finally how to ride a bike.

Guided Practice

Practice using proofreading marks with this paragraph.

I wore a helmut and wore it for safety. I practicd riding

my bike a lot. It took a long time. I finally learnd finally how

to ride. my brother will now let me try riding her bike.

 Did you find the mistakes? Here are the correct answers:

UNIT 1 ▓▓▓▓▓▓▓▓▓▓▓▓▓▓▓▓▓▓▓▓▓▓▓▓▓▓▓▓▓▓▓▓▓
Elements of Writing

© The Continental Press, Inc.   DUPLICATING THIS MATERIAL IS ILLEGAL.

Change <u>helmut</u> to <u>helmet</u> in sentence 1.
Take out <u>and wore it</u> in sentence 1.
Change <u>practicd</u> to <u>practiced</u> in sentence 2.
Change <u>learnd</u> to <u>learned</u> and take out the second
<u>finally</u> in sentence 4.
Change <u>my</u> to <u>My</u> and change <u>her</u> to <u>his</u> in sentence 5.

Look at the draft below with its proofreading
corrections. Can you identify them? You should find four
more proofreading corrections. Make the corrections on
the draft.

When I was 5, I wanted a bike to ride like my brother.

He had a Santa cruz. ~~It was a~~ mountain bike. my bike was

and
small. It had training wheels on it. All of my friends could

their
ride ~~there~~ bikes. I did not no how to ride a real ~~good~~ bike. I

asked my dad to teach me. He said I had to learn how to

ride mine first. ~~Before I could ride a mountain bike.~~ It was

Turning
hard to learn. I felt left out. I fell down a lot corners was

my bike
hard. I fell once when I hit a rock. My dad he said he would

alongside
help me balance. He held the bike and ran, I wore a helmet.

~~It is~~ for safety. I practiced a lot. ~~It took a long time,~~ and I

finally learnd how. My dad ~~he~~ said maybe next year I can get

a mountain bike.

© The Continental Press, Inc. DUPLICATING THIS MATERIAL IS ILLEGAL.

Did you find all the corrections? Here are the correct answers:

> Change <u>cruz</u> to <u>Cruz</u> in sentence 2.
> Change <u>no</u> to <u>know</u> in sentence 6.
> Take out the word <u>he</u> after <u>dad</u> in sentence 13.
> Change <u>learnd</u> to <u>learned</u> in sentence 16.

Step 5: Publishing

Once you have fixed any mistakes or problems with your work, you are ready to publish it. **Publishing** means to share your work with other people. This is the last stage of writing. You might turn in your paper to your teacher. Or, you may read it to the class. Maybe, you will create a poster with your work. Publishing can take many forms.

© The Continental Press, Inc.   DUPLICATING THIS MATERIAL IS ILLEGAL.

Test Yourself

> Write a story about learning to use the computer. What did you learn first? Was it easy or hard to learn? What kind of activity did you learn to do? When writing your story, be sure to include:
>
> • a title for your story
>
> • a beginning, middle, and end to your story
>
> • details to make your story interesting

1 What are you being asked to write about?

_____

_____

_____

_____

_____

Read
Note
Organize

© The Continental Press, Inc.   DUPLICATING THIS MATERIAL IS ILLEGAL.

2 Use this story map to plan your story.

Details

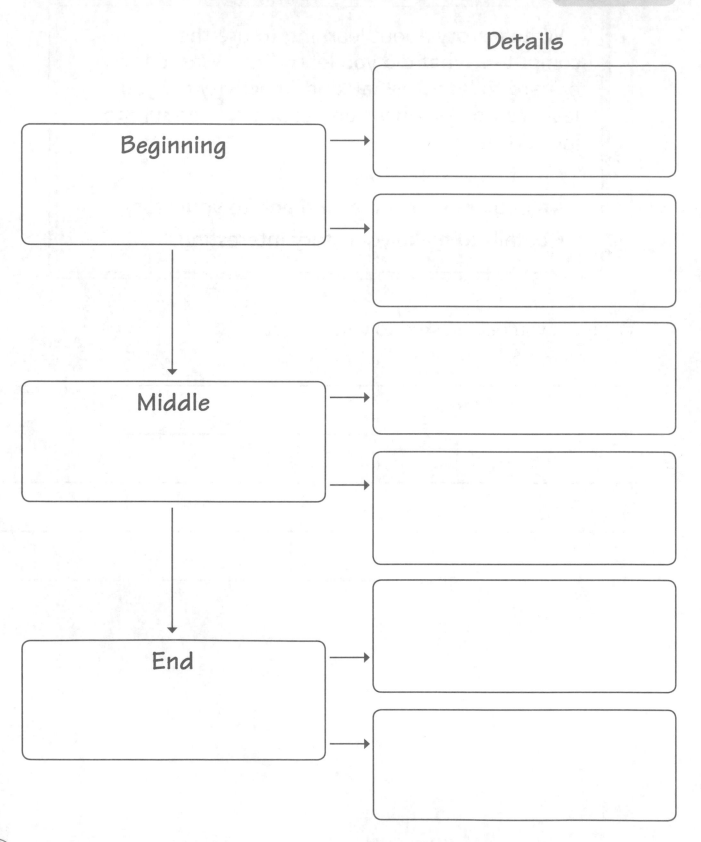

Beginning

Middle

End

UNIT 1
Elements of Writing

© The Continental Press, Inc.   DUPLICATING THIS MATERIAL IS ILLEGAL.

3 You have thought about the topic of your story. You have also planned your ideas. Now, write a draft of your story. Your draft should describe how you learned to use the computer. Use details to make your story clear.

_____

_____

_____

_____

_____

_____

_____

_____

_____

_____

_____

_____

© The Continental Press, Inc.   DUPLICATING THIS MATERIAL IS ILLEGAL.

4 You have written your draft. Now, read it again carefully. Change ideas if you need to. Next, edit your draft. Check for mistakes in spelling, capitalization, and punctuation. Make corrections on your draft. Use the checklist on page 15 to review your writing. Have a classmate edit your writing if necessary.

_____

_____

_____

_____

_____

_____

_____

_____

_____

_____

_____

© The Continental Press, Inc. DUPLICATING THIS MATERIAL IS ILLEGAL.

5 Then write your final answer on the lines below.
Publish your work by showing it to your teacher.

_____

_____

_____

_____

_____

_____

_____

_____

_____

_____

_____

_____

© The Continental Press, Inc.   DUPLICATING THIS MATERIAL IS ILLEGAL.

Writing a Paragraph

W.2.2, 5, 6

A good paragraph has one important idea. It is called the **main idea.** All of the sentences in the paragraph should be about this idea. The **topic sentence** should tell what the main idea is. This sentence is usually the first sentence of the paragraph. The other sentences give details or facts about the main idea.

Guided Practice

Read the paragraphs. Then answer the questions.

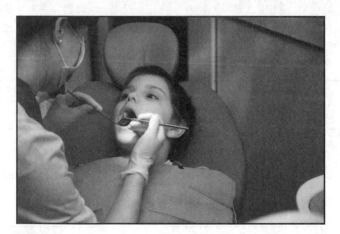

Some children are afraid to go to the dentist, but there are many interesting things to learn there. The dentist will tell you all about your teeth. He will tell you how to take care of them. You will learn the best way to brush and floss your teeth. The dentist uses noisy tools to clean your teeth. They will not hurt you. You might also get an x-ray. The dentist looks at the x-ray. He is checking to see if you have a cavity inside a tooth. The dentist may fill the cavity. But the dentist will make sure that this does not hurt.

© The Continental Press, Inc. DUPLICATING THIS MATERIAL IS ILLEGAL.

Which is the topic sentence in the paragraph?

A sentence 1

B sentence 2

C sentence 3

D sentence 4

The topic sentence gives you an idea of what the whole paragraph is about. It does not need to be the first sentence. It can be any sentence. However, often it is the first sentence. Choice A is the correct answer. This is the topic sentence. Choices B, C, and D are incorrect.

Topic: Gardens

_____

_____

 Some people only like to grow flowers. Others only grow vegetables and fruits. Many people have small kitchen gardens with herb plants. They use herb plants in cooking. Some people do not have a yard. They plant their gardens in window boxes. A garden must be in a sunny spot. Plants need lots of sun to grow. Of course, if you have a rock garden, you won't need any sun at all.

Write a topic sentence for the paragraph.

_____

_____

First, look at the topic. Then read the paragraph. What is the main idea? What is the subject of the paragraph? Here is a sample answer:

There are many different types of gardens.

© The Continental Press, Inc.   DUPLICATING THIS MATERIAL IS ILLEGAL.

Organizing the Paragraph

Every sentence in a paragraph should be about the subject. This chart shows the order of the sentences in the paragraph about going to the dentist on page 24.

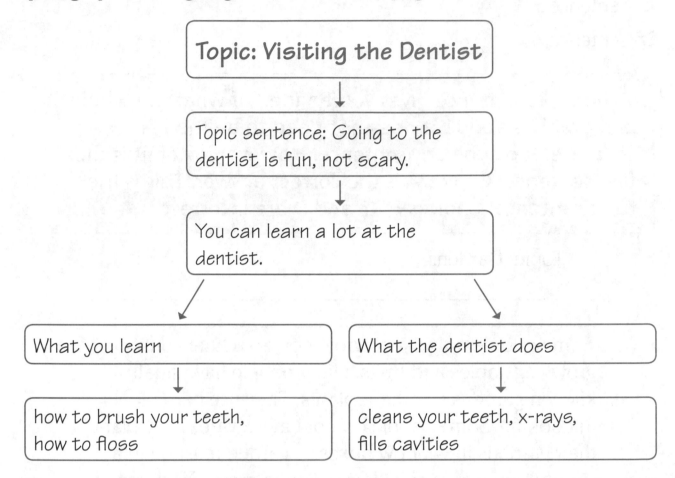

A paragraph should end with a **closing sentence.** This sentence sums up the paragraph. It tells something final about the topic.

© The Continental Press, Inc.   DUPLICATING THIS MATERIAL IS ILLEGAL.

Guided Practice

_____ You can run, jump, or play ball to exercise.

_____ Everyone should exercise a little bit each day.

_____ Exercise is important to stay healthy.

_____ There are many types of exercise.

_____

_____

_____

_____

✓ **What is the paragraph about? Decide which sentence is the topic sentence. Then number the sentences in the order you will use them. Here is a sample answer:**

_3_ You can run, jump, or play ball to exercise.

_4_ Everyone should exercise a little bit each day.

_1_ Exercise is important to stay healthy.

_2_ There are many types of exercise.

Exercise is important to stay healthy. There are many types of exercise. You can run, jump, or play ball to exercise. Everyone should exercise a little bit each day. That way, we can all stay healthy.

© The Continental Press, Inc. DUPLICATING THIS MATERIAL IS ILLEGAL.

There are many ways to set up a paragraph. Which order will you choose? It depends on the kind of writing you are doing. Here are some ways to put information in order.

Sometimes, you write a paragraph to explain something. You can do this in two ways. You can give **details** that support your main idea. The paragraph on visiting the dentist gives this kind of detail. The second way is to give **examples** of the main idea. The paragraph on gardens gives examples.

Use **time order** when you write a story. You need to tell the events in the order that they happened. Connecting words and phrases help you put things in time order. Use words such as <u>first</u>, <u>then</u>, <u>after that</u>, <u>later</u>, and <u>finally</u>.

Use **location** when you are describing a scene. Explain where things are in your description. If you want to describe a new park, you might use connecting words and phrases, such as <u>close by</u>, <u>far away</u>, or <u>around</u>.

Look at these words and phrases. They can help you describe a scene or location.

across	beside	close by	next to
behind	between	near	in front of

© The Continental Press, Inc.   DUPLICATING THIS MATERIAL IS ILLEGAL.

Guided Practice

Look around your classroom. Where do you sit? Who or what is near you? Write a short paragraph describing where you sit in your classroom. Use the words on page 28 to help you write your paragraph.

_____

_____

_____

 Help the reader see what you see. Do you sit next to a window? Are you between two students? Here is a sample answer:

My desk is in front of Mrs. Lentz. Cara sits next to me.
I am the first one in the row. My desk is next to a window.
The door is across the room from me. Tyrone sits behind me.

Writing for a Test

Sometimes, you must write a short answer to a question on a test. Your answer should be a paragraph. Use these steps to write your answer in the time you are given.

1. Underline the key words. This will help you understand the question.
2. Think about what you want to say.
3. Decide which plan you will use to set up your paragraph.
4. Write your topic sentence first. Then finish your paragraph.
5. Check your answer. You can still make changes.

© The Continental Press, Inc. DUPLICATING THIS MATERIAL IS ILLEGAL.

Guided Practice

Read this article about board games. Then read the test question.

Let's Play!

You can make up a game if you just have a flat space and a few things to use as game pieces. People have been doing this since the beginning of history! Board games have been around for thousands of years. The oldest board game may be an Egyptian game called Senet. Another very old board game is the Chinese game called Go.

Many children's first game is Chutes and Ladders or Candyland. A popular game for the whole family is Monopoly. In all of these games, you roll dice. The number that comes up tells you how many spaces to move your game piece. Then the place you land on tells you what to do next.

In some board games, you try to reach the end of a path first. In games like checkers, you try to capture the other player's pieces. In games like Monopoly or Risk, you try to get the most land or the most money. It's always exciting to win. But most of all, the best part is having fun!

© The Continental Press, Inc. DUPLICATING THIS MATERIAL IS ILLEGAL.

> Write a paragraph about board games you know how to play. Tell about the first board game you played. Then tell about other board games that you like to play now. In your answer be sure to:
> - include a topic sentence stating your main idea
> - use time order to tell the events

Here is how one student, Xander, wrote his answer. First, he underlined important parts of the question. Then he made some notes. He knew he would need to write about his own experience. He planned to use time order to set up the events in his paragraph.

Read
Note
Organize

To plan his writing, Xander wrote down the events that he wanted to tell. Then he listed them in the order in which they happened. Here is what he wrote:

Read
Note
Organize

1. The first board game I ever played was Candyland
2. I was 4 years old when I played it
3. Then I learned to play Battleship
4. Now I play Monopoly with my brother
5. I always pick the racecar piece
6. My brother always wins

Xander finished his plan. Then he used the events that he listed to write his paragraph.

© The Continental Press, Inc.   DUPLICATING THIS MATERIAL IS ILLEGAL.

I have loved to play board games ever since I was a little boy. When I was 4 years old, I learned to play Candyland. It was the first time I ever played a board game. I loved the candy cards. The next game I played was Battleship. It was harder to win that one. Now, I play Monopoly with my brother. I always pick the racecar piece. No matter how many times I play, my brother beats me. If I keep playing, I know I will beat him someday.

Circle the words in the paragraph that show time order.

 Time order tells what happened first, next, and last. Did you find all the words? Here is the correct answer:

When, first, next, Now, someday

Underline Xander's topic sentence.

 The topic sentence tells the main idea. Here is the correct answer:

I have loved playing board games ever since I was a little boy.

© The Continental Press, Inc. DUPLICATING THIS MATERIAL IS ILLEGAL.

Test Yourself

Circle the letter of the sentence in each group that would make the best topic sentence of a paragraph.

1   A   Cats and dogs are popular animals to have as pets.

    B   There are many different breeds of dogs.

    C   Cats can have short hair or long hair.

    D   Some dogs are easier to train than others.

2   A   The lunch program will stop selling soda.

    B   Pizza will be on the menu.

    C   The school cafeteria is getting a new menu.

    D   Lunches will cost more money.

3   A   Soy milk is another good source of protein.

    B   Children should drink two or three glasses of milk a day.

    C   Some children cannot drink regular milk.

    D   Milk is an important food for children and adults.

4   A   Many children and adults like to skateboard in Greendale Park.

    B   Some people want to set up a skateboarding park there.

    C   It is important to dress for safety when you skateboard.

    D   Walkers in the park say that skateboarders sometimes crash into them.

© The Continental Press, Inc.   DUPLICATING THIS MATERIAL IS ILLEGAL.

5 Read the question. Then write a paragraph.

The article on page 30 ends: "It's always exciting to win. But most of all, the best part is having fun!" Write a paragraph telling what this means. Be sure to:

• include a topic sentence that tells your main idea

• use details to back it up

_____

_____

_____

_____

_____

_____

_____

_____

_____

_____

_____

© The Continental Press, Inc.   DUPLICATING THIS MATERIAL IS ILLEGAL.

Main Idea and Details

W.2.2, 5, 6

The **main idea** is what the text is about. The **details** support the text. Or, they explain more about the main idea.

Guided Practice

Read the passage. Then answer the questions.

The Story of Marbles

Children all over the world play games with marbles. These games are fun and easy. Best of all, you can always carry the game in your pocket! Did you know that children have been playing marbles for thousands of years?

The oldest marbles were found in ancient Egypt. They were more than 3,000 years old and were made of clay. People in ancient Rome also played marbles.

© The Continental Press, Inc.   DUPLICATING THIS MATERIAL IS ILLEGAL.

Marbles more than 2,000 years old have been found in Mexico. In the 1800s, toy companies started making marbles. They sold thousands and thousands of them. Some were made of marble stone, which gave marbles their name.

Now, marbles are made of glass. They come in many sizes and colors. There are a lot of different games to play with marbles. A popular one is to hit the other person's marble with your own. Then you win their marbles. Another game is to roll the marble through a hoop or into a hole. You can flick it with your thumb. This is called knuckling. Or, you can roll it with your hand.

Marbles are a lot of fun to play, whichever game you choose. They are beautiful to look at, too. Many people collect them because they are so pretty. Now that you know more about marbles, grab a handful and go play!

You have just joined the marbles club at your school. You are going to write an article about playing the game for the school newsletter. Be sure to include:

- a main idea about marbles
- facts and details from the article that support the main idea

---

© The Continental Press, Inc.   DUPLICATING THIS MATERIAL IS ILLEGAL.

Step 1: Prewriting

Read
Note
Organize

Now, you will see how one student, Jade, answered the question. She used facts and details from the article.

Jade knew she had to read the question more than once. She underlined important words and made notes.

What key words do you think Jade underlined?

_____

_____

The key words help you know what you will write about. Here is a sample answer:

> Jade underlined the words <u>article</u>, <u>newsletter</u>, <u>main idea</u>, and <u>facts and details</u>.

Jade read the question again. Then she looked back at the article. This time she took notes. Here are her notes:

Read
Note
Organize

> Topic: marbles
> I will write for other students.
> Marbles fit in your pocket.
> It is fun and easy.
> Marbles are pretty and people collect them.
> There are a few ways to play.

© The Continental Press, Inc.   DUPLICATING THIS MATERIAL IS ILLEGAL.

First, you need to understand the question. Then you can plan your writing. Jade decided to use a web to help her plan. She wrote her main idea in the center.

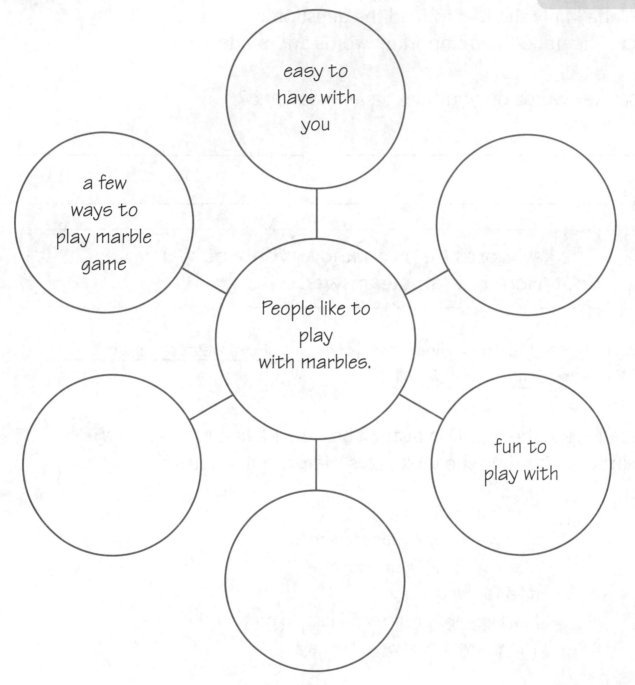

© The Continental Press, Inc.   DUPLICATING THIS MATERIAL IS ILLEGAL.

Which details support Jade's main idea? Check the items
that fit into the web.

_____ Marbles are colorful and pretty.

_____ Ancient Egyptians liked to play games.

_____ People dig for artifacts in Mexico.

_____ Marbles fit in your pocket.

✓ The main idea is that people like to play with marbles.
The details should tell why this is so. Here are the correct
answers:

__✓__ Marbles are colorful and pretty.

_____ Ancient Egyptians liked to play games.

_____ People dig for artifacts in Mexico.

__✓__ Marbles fit in your pocket.

The next step is for Jade to write her draft.

© The Continental Press, Inc.   DUPLICATING THIS MATERIAL IS ILLEGAL.

Step 2: Drafting

People everywhere enjoy playing games with marbles. Marbles have been used since ancient times. Marbles are made of glass and come in different sizes. They come in lots of colors, too. Playing marbles is fun and easy. They are always handy. Because you can carry them in your pocket! There are few ways to play marbles. you can try to hit the other person marble. Then you get to keep it. In another game you try to get your marbles into a hole or a hoop. Some people play games with marbles. Others like two collect marbles because they are so pretty.

Underline the topic sentence in the draft.

 The topic sentence gives the main idea. It is often the first sentence. However, it is not always the first sentence. Here is the correct answer:

I underlined the sentence <u>People everywhere enjoy playing games with marbles.</u>

© The Continental Press, Inc. DUPLICATING THIS MATERIAL IS ILLEGAL.

How many marble games did Jade write about?

_____

_____

✓ How does Jade support her main idea? Think about the details she gives. Here is a sample answer:

Jade wrote about two marble games.

Why did she tell about these games?

_____

_____

✓ Think about what the question asked. What is the reason for writing? Here is a sample answer:

Jade told about these games because the question asked her to write about marble games.

© The Continental Press, Inc.   DUPLICATING THIS MATERIAL IS ILLEGAL.

Read the revised draft carefully. Then answer the questions.

People everywhere enjoy playing games with marbles. ~~Marbles have been used since ancient times.~~ Marbles are made of glass and come in different sizes. They come in lots of colors, too. Playing marbles is fun and easy. They are always handy. Because you can carry them in your pocket! There are a few ways to play marbles. you can try to hit the other person's marble. Then you get to keep it. In another game you try to get your marbles into a hole or a hoop. Some people play games with marbles. Others like two collect marbles because they are so pretty.

Why did Jade take out sentence 2?

_____

_____

 All the sentences in a paragraph should tell about the main idea. The facts and details should support the main idea. Here is a sample answer:

Jade took it out because it was not about the main idea. The main idea is playing games with marbles.

© The Continental Press, Inc. DUPLICATING THIS MATERIAL IS ILLEGAL.

Underline the words that Jade made part of another sentence. Why did she make these words part of the sentence that came before them?

_____

_____

A sentence must have a subject and a predicate. Sentences that do not have both a subject or predicate should be taken out. Or, they should be rewritten. Here is a sample answer:

I underlined <u>Because you can carry them in your pocket!</u> Jade added these words to another sentence. She did this because they do not make a complete sentence.

Peer Review

Jade might exchange papers with another student. They would review each other's work. Then they would give it a score based on the checklist, or rubric. They would discuss ways to improve their work.

© The Continental Press, Inc.   DUPLICATING THIS MATERIAL IS ILLEGAL.

Checklist for Writing Main Idea and Details

Score 3
- The writing answers all parts of the question.
- The writing includes a clear main idea.
- The writing includes important details that go with the main idea.
- Words are used correctly and well.
- Capitalization and punctuation are correct.

Score 2
- The writing answers almost all parts of the question.
- The main idea is not completely clear.
- The writing mostly sticks to the topic but there are some details that don't belong.
- Some words are not used correctly.
- There are some mistakes in capitalization and punctuation.

Score 1
- The writing answers only part of the question.
- There is no main idea.
- The writing is missing important details.
- Many words are overused or not used correctly.
- There are many mistakes in capitalization and punctuation.

Now, Jade is ready to edit her revised draft.

© The Continental Press, Inc.   DUPLICATING THIS MATERIAL IS ILLEGAL.

Step 4: Editing

_____

_____

 Look for misspelled words and misplaced punctuation. Did you find all the mistakes? Here are the correct answers:

Capitalize the word you so it is You in sentence 7.

Change the word two so it is to in the last sentence.

Step 5: Publishing

Jade published her paper by turning in her paper to the teacher.

© The Continental Press, Inc.   DUPLICATING THIS MATERIAL IS ILLEGAL.

Questions and Answers About Marbles

Q. What are marbles made of?

A. Marbles used to be made of clay. They were also made from marble or stone. Some were even made from wood or seeds! Now, marbles are made from glass.

Q. What's the difference between sizes of marbles?

A. The peewee is the smallest marble. Then there is the regular size. Then there are shooters, which are about an inch wide. They are used to hit smaller marbles.

Q. How do I play marbles?

A. There are many ways to play. One game is called Bun-Hole. Dig a hole in the ground. Stand ten feet away from the hole. Shoot your marble as close to the hole as you can get. But don't let it go in the hole! You can knock the other player's marble into the hole. The player who gets his or her marbles closest to the hole takes a marble from the other players. Another game is the opposite. You try to get your marble into the hole!

Q. If I lose, do I really have to give up my marbles?

A. Some people play "for fair." This means that each person gets to take back their marbles after playing. But some play "for keeps." This means that if you lose your marbles in a game, you don't get them back. You and the other players can make the rules for your games. Just make sure you agree before you play!

© The Continental Press, Inc.   DUPLICATING THIS MATERIAL IS ILLEGAL.

You have decided to give your best friend marbles for a birthday gift. Write a note to go with the gift. Tell your friend how to play a game of marbles. Be sure to include:

- a main idea
- important details for playing the game

1 What kind of writing are you being asked to do?

Read
Note
Organize

_____

_____

_____

_____

2 What will your writing look like when you are done? (Hint: One sentence? Two paragraphs?)

_____

_____

_____

_____

_____

© The Continental Press, Inc.   DUPLICATING THIS MATERIAL IS ILLEGAL.

3 Who will read your writing?

_____

_____

_____

_____

_____

© The Continental Press, Inc.   DUPLICATING THIS MATERIAL IS ILLEGAL.

4 Fill in the idea web below. This will help you answer the question.

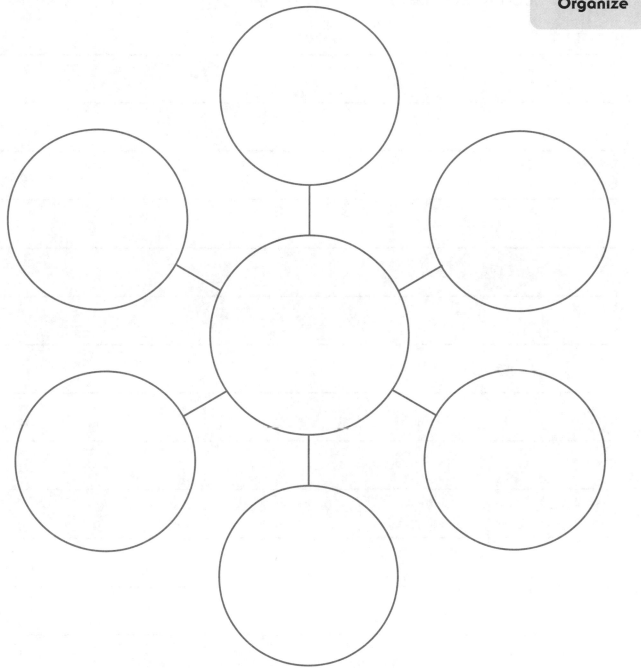

© The Continental Press, Inc.   DUPLICATING THIS MATERIAL IS ILLEGAL.

5 Now, write your draft. Look at your plan. Think about a topic sentence. Are all your ideas in order? Do you need to add details?

_____

_____

_____

_____

_____

_____

_____

_____

_____

_____

_____

_____

_____

_____

© The Continental Press, Inc.   DUPLICATING THIS MATERIAL IS ILLEGAL.

6 When you have finished your draft, go back over it. Make your changes on this page. Check your draft for mistakes. Use the checklist on page 44. Ask a classmate to edit your work if your teacher says to do so.

_____

_____

_____

_____

_____

_____

_____

_____

_____

_____

_____

_____

© The Continental Press, Inc.   DUPLICATING THIS MATERIAL IS ILLEGAL.

7 Write your final answer on this page. Publish it by showing it to your teacher.

_____

_____

_____

_____

_____

_____

_____

_____

_____

_____

_____

_____

_____

© The Continental Press, Inc.   DUPLICATING THIS MATERIAL IS ILLEGAL.

Cause and Effect

W.2.2, 5, 6

A **cause** is <u>why</u> something happens. An **effect** is <u>what</u> happens because of the cause. For example, a glass dropped on the floor is a cause. The effect is that it breaks. You most likely see how ideas and events are related when you read. Your reading makes more sense when you understand these why connections. Clue words signal causes. These words are <u>because</u>, <u>since</u>, and <u>due to</u>. Words that are clues to effects are <u>then</u>, <u>so</u>, and <u>as a result</u>.

Guided Practice

Read the story. Then answer the questions.

Open for Business

Raccoon and Squirrel decided to make some money. On market day, Raccoon set up a peanut stand. Squirrel set up an ice-cream stand. They both waited for customers.

Squirrel asked Raccoon, "How much are you charging for a bag of peanuts?"

Raccoon replied, "One penny." Squirrel took out a penny and bought a bag of peanuts from Raccoon. Squirrel gobbled them all.

A little while later, Raccoon inquired, "How much for a cup of ice cream?"

© The Continental Press, Inc.   DUPLICATING THIS MATERIAL IS ILLEGAL.

"A penny," said Squirrel. Raccoon paid with the penny. He slurped the ice cream fast.

Then Squirrel used the penny to buy another bag of peanuts. And shortly after that, Raccoon bought another cup of ice cream from Squirrel.

Back and forth they went, each buying the other's treat with the penny. By the end of the day, Squirrel and Raccoon had no more treats to sell.

"I can't understand it!" said Raccoon. "I sold all of my peanuts, but I have only one penny."

"What about me?" said Squirrel. "I started out the day with a penny, and now it's gone. And my ice cream is gone, too!"

The friends headed home, their bellies full. Both wondered how they could have sold all their treats and yet have made no money.

© The Continental Press, Inc.   DUPLICATING THIS MATERIAL IS ILLEGAL.

The story "Open for Business" tells what happens when Raccoon and Squirrel try to sell treats to make money. At the end of the story, they can't figure out why they haven't made any money. Write a note to Squirrel and Raccoon. Explain why they didn't make any money. In your note, be sure to include:

- the reason they made no money
- the reason they have no treats left
- the word <u>because</u>

Step 1: Prewriting

Let's look at how one student, Drew, answered the question. He used details from the story to write an answer to the question. The first thing Drew did was read the question slowly and carefully.

Then he read it again. This time he underlined the important parts. He wanted to know what he was to write.

Read
Note
Organize

© The Continental Press, Inc.   DUPLICATING THIS MATERIAL IS ILLEGAL.

Which of these do you think Drew underlined?

A Write a note to Squirrel and Raccoon.

B The story "Open for Business" tells what happens when Raccoon and Squirrel try to sell treats to make money.

C At the end of the story, they can't figure out why they haven't made any money.

D In your note, be sure to include:

Choice A is the only one that explains what Drew is to write. He is to write a note. Choice A is the correct answer. Choices B, C, and D do not tell what Drew should write. They are incorrect.

Explain what other important parts Drew underlined.

_____

_____

_____

_____

Think about what the note will explain. What are the causes? What are the effects? Here is a sample answer:

    Drew underlined the sentence <u>Explain why they didn't make any money.</u> He also underlined <u>the reason they made no money.</u> He underlined <u>the reason they have no treats left</u> and <u>the word because.</u>

© The Continental Press, Inc. DUPLICATING THIS MATERIAL IS ILLEGAL.

Next, Drew made notes about what to write. Here is what he wrote:

Read
Note
Organize

I will write a note to Squirrel and Raccoon

explain why they have no money

explain why they have no treats left

use the word <u>because</u>

Drew understood that he was writing a note to explain reasons, or **causes.** He read the story again to find the details he needed. He drew this chart to show the reasons to include in his note to Squirrel and Raccoon.

Read
Note
Organize

Reasons (Causes)
1. Raccoon and Squirrel had just one penny.
2. They kept trading it.
3. Raccoon ate up all of Squirrel's ice cream.
4. Squirrel ate up all of Raccoon's peanuts.
5. They didn't sell any treats to customers.

What Happened (Effects)
1. They made no money.
2. They had no treats left.

© The Continental Press, Inc.   DUPLICATING THIS MATERIAL IS ILLEGAL.

Drew knew that in a note to the story characters, he should use the words <u>you</u>, <u>your</u>, and <u>yourselves</u>. He wrote a first sentence about why the story characters made no money. Here is what Drew wrote:

> You thought you were selling your treats, but you really weren't.

If you were starting a note to Raccoon and Squirrel, what would you write as a first sentence?

_____

_____

 The first sentence should tell why you are writing. It is like the topic sentence in a story or passage. It tells the main idea. Here is a sample answer:

> You say that you can't understand why you made no money, but I can explain why.

Drew's next step is to use his graphic organizer to write his draft.

© The Continental Press, Inc.   DUPLICATING THIS MATERIAL IS ILLEGAL.

Step 2: Drafting

Dear Raccoon and Squirrel,

You thought you were selling your treats, but you weren't really. You didn't make any money because you kept trading the same penny back and forth. You had no treats left! Next time if you want to make money, you can't sell you're treats just to each other. You have to sell too other customers.

Two effects are listed in Drew's note. Find them and underline them in Drew's note.

 Effects are the result of something that happened. Here is the correct answer:

Cause 1: You didn't make any money.
Cause 2: You had no treats left.

© The Continental Press, Inc.   DUPLICATING THIS MATERIAL IS ILLEGAL.

What did Drew explain as the reason why Raccoon and Squirrel did not make any money?

_____

_____

_____

> The word __because__ lets a reader know that something is about to be explained. Did Drew use this word in his note? This will help you understand the cause. Here is a sample answer:

Drew explains that the reason they made no money is because they kept trading the same penny back and forth.

Now, Drew is ready to revise his draft.

© The Continental Press, Inc.   DUPLICATING THIS MATERIAL IS ILLEGAL.

Step 3: Revising

Dear Raccoon and Squirrel,

You thought you were selling your treats, but you
The reason   is
weren't really. You didn't make any money because you

kept trading the same penny back and forth. You had no
because you ate them all yourselves.
treats left! Next time, if you want to make money, you

can't sell you're treats just to each other. You have to sell
Good luck next time!
too other customers.

Your friend,

Drew

Drew wrote the sentence, "You had no treats left!" Why
did he add words to that sentence?

_____

_____

✓ The sentence tells about something that happened.
Here is a sample answer:

He added words to explain the cause and to answer the
question completely.

© The Continental Press, Inc.   DUPLICATING THIS MATERIAL IS ILLEGAL.

What did Drew add to make the writing seem like a note to friends?

_____

_____

 Think about how you talk to your friends. Do you greet them? Do you say goodbye? Here is a sample answer:

He wished them good luck. Then he put a closing and a signature.

Peer Review

Drew used a checklist to review his writing. This checklist is also called a rubric. Then he traded papers with another student. They gave each other a score based on the checklist. Then they talked about ways to make their writing better.

© The Continental Press, Inc.   DUPLICATING THIS MATERIAL IS ILLEGAL.

Checklist for Writing Cause and Effect

Score 3

- The writing answers all parts of the question.
- The writing has three or more sentences.
- The writing clearly explains the problem and its cause.
- The writing uses the word <u>because</u> correctly.
- The writing stays on the subject.
- Capitalization and punctuation are correct.

Score 2

- The writing answers almost all of the question.
- The writing has two or three sentences.
- The writing explains the problem and its cause.
- The writing uses the word <u>because</u> correctly.
- The writing includes details that are not about the subject.
- There are some mistakes in capitalization and punctuation.

Score 1

- The writing answers only part of the question.
- The writing has two or fewer sentences.
- The writing does not explain the problem or the cause.
- The word <u>because</u> is not used correctly.
- It is hard to tell what the subject is.
- There are many mistakes in capitalization and punctuation.

Drew's next step is to edit his work.

© The Continental Press, Inc.   DUPLICATING THIS MATERIAL IS ILLEGAL.

Step 4: Editing

Read the revised draft again. Find and correct two more mistakes.

Mistake 1: _____

Mistake 2: _____

Before you turn in a paper there is one more step. Now is the time to proofread your work. You are looking for mistakes. A period might be missing. Sometimes, a word is misspelled. Here is the correct answer:

Mistake 1: Change the word you're to the word your.

Mistake 2: Change the word too to the word to.

The last step is for Drew to publish his work.

Step 5: Publishing

You publish something by sharing it with others. These could be your friends, your teacher, or your class. Drew is now ready to publish his note. He can do this by turning in his note to the teacher.

© The Continental Press, Inc.   DUPLICATING THIS MATERIAL IS ILLEGAL.

Chipmunk in the Storeroom

Chipmunk was very hungry. She had not eaten in a week, and she was as thin as a ribbon. When she spied a small hole in the outer wall of a farm building, she squeezed through it. What a wonderful sight she came upon! Here was a storeroom filled with sacks of grain!

Chipmunk began eating. She nibbled and gnawed and gobbled the grain. She ate and ate, taking only a few minutes to rest between meals.

After several days of eating, Chipmunk was napping. A sudden noise woke her up. She raced to the hole to escape. But she couldn't find the hole. Around and around she spun, but the only hole she found was too small for her. She could barely push her head out.

"What happened to the hole I came in through?" she asked Mouse, who was passing by outside.

"You're in it. At least, your head is in it," Mouse answered. "Remember that you entered with an empty belly. You must leave the same way."

© The Continental Press, Inc.   DUPLICATING THIS MATERIAL IS ILLEGAL.

The story "Chipmunk in the Storeroom" tells what happens when Chipmunk eats from the sacks of grain in the storeroom. At the end of the story, she has a problem. Write three or more sentences to explain the problem. In your sentences, be sure to include:

- what Chipmunk's problem is
- why she has a problem
- the word <u>because</u>

1 What kind of writing will you do?

Read
Note
Organize

_____

_____

_____

_____

_____

2 What could you point out with the word <u>because</u>?

_____

_____

_____

_____

_____

_____

© The Continental Press, Inc.   DUPLICATING THIS MATERIAL IS ILLEGAL.

3 Show how you will plan your sentences. Fill in the chart. Then answer the question.

> **Reasons (Causes)**

> **What Happened (Effects)**

What should you tell about in your first sentence?

_____

_____

_____

_____

© The Continental Press, Inc. DUPLICATING THIS MATERIAL IS ILLEGAL.

4 Write a draft of your sentences. Use your chart and idea about a first sentence. Remember to include the needed details and special word.

_____

_____

_____

_____

_____

_____

_____

_____

_____

_____

_____

_____

© The Continental Press, Inc.   DUPLICATING THIS MATERIAL IS ILLEGAL.

5 When you have finished your draft, read it carefully. Rewrite your changes on this page. Proofread for mistakes. Use the checklist on page 63 to look over your work. Have a classmate edit your writing if the teacher says to do so.

_____

_____

_____

_____

_____

_____

_____

_____

_____

_____

_____

_____

_____

© The Continental Press, Inc.   DUPLICATING THIS MATERIAL IS ILLEGAL.

6 Write your final copy below. Publish your work by showing it to your teacher.

_____

_____

_____

_____

_____

_____

_____

_____

_____

_____

_____

_____

_____

© The Continental Press, Inc.   DUPLICATING THIS MATERIAL IS ILLEGAL.

Compare and Contrast

W.2.2, 5, 6

Sometimes, you will be asked to tell how two things are the same. This is called **comparing.** You might also be asked how they are different. This is called **contrasting.**

Guided Practice

Read the passage. Then answer the questions.

from "Lucas's Medal"

Lucas sat on the bench. It was Zoe's turn to skate. Lucas had to wait. Soon, it would be his turn. He was nervous. But Zoe made it look so easy. She was a good jumper. Why couldn't Lucas jump like his sister? Lucas pressed his skates into the floor. He tried not to watch Zoe. Maybe then, he wouldn't be so afraid.

Zoe was good at everything. She was first in her class in reading. She was good in math, too. She could dance well. She never got scared. And today, she would get a skating medal. Many things were hard for Lucas. He had a hard time in school. Reading was not easy for him. He wanted to do better. But sometimes letters just didn't look right. Sometimes, he felt

© The Continental Press, Inc.   DUPLICATING THIS MATERIAL IS ILLEGAL.

like giving up. Still, Zoe always cheered him on. She was his biggest fan. If Zoe cheered, Lucas felt less scared. Maybe today he would get a medal.

The bell rang for the next skater to come on the ice. It was Lucas's turn! He had been too busy thinking. He didn't notice the time. Now, he had to get on the ice. Zoe cheered and waved. "Go, Lucas! You can do it!" Lucas glided onto the ice. His hands were shaking. But he knew he had to try.

Stories are interesting when two characters are different. It is also interesting to see ways that they are alike. Write a paragraph or more about Lucas and Zoe, in "Lucas's Medal." Show how Lucas and Zoe are alike. Then, show how they are different. In your answer, use details from the story that show:

- ways the two characters are alike
- ways the two characters are different

© The Continental Press, Inc. DUPLICATING THIS MATERIAL IS ILLEGAL.

Step 1: Prewriting

This is how one student named Eric answered the question. He began by reading the question very carefully. He kept reading it until he understood what to write.

He underlined important points as he read. He underlined

- the subject
- what to write about
- the kind of writing

Which of these is the subject that Eric underlined?

A Stories are interesting

B a paragraph or more

C Lucas and Zoe

D details from the story

The subject is Lucas and Zoe. This is what Eric will write about. Choice C is the correct answer. Choices A, B, and D are not the subject. These are incorrect.

© The Continental Press, Inc.   DUPLICATING THIS MATERIAL IS ILLEGAL.

What will Eric write about?

_____

_____

_____

_____

 The subject is Lucas and Zoe. The question asks what Eric will write about his subject. What did he underline? Here is a sample answer:

> Eric will write about how Lucas and Zoe are alike. He will also write about how Zoe and Lucas are not alike. He underlined ways that the two characters are alike. He also underlined ways that the two characters are different.

Eric underlined the kind of writing. What did he underline in the question?

A a paragraph or more

B use details to show

C It is also interesting

D In your answer

 The question tells what form the writing should take. Choice A is the correct answer. Eric underlined a paragraph or more. Choices B, C, and D are incorrect.

© The Continental Press, Inc.   DUPLICATING THIS MATERIAL IS ILLEGAL.

Eric read the question. Who are the characters in the story? What did he have to write about? Eric wrote down his ideas. He made the Venn diagram below.

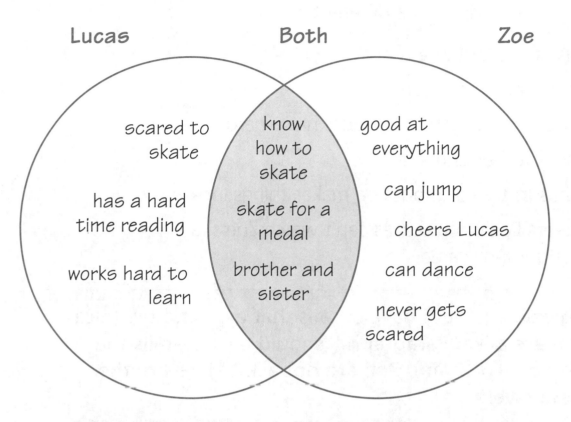

Lucas   Both   Zoe

scared to skate

has a hard time reading

works hard to learn

know how to skate

skate for a medal

brother and sister

good at everything

can jump

cheers Lucas

can dance

never gets scared

Next, Eric organized his alike and different writing. He wrote his answer in two paragraphs. His first paragraph will tell how Lucas and Zoe are alike. His second paragraph will tell how they are different.

© The Continental Press, Inc.   DUPLICATING THIS MATERIAL IS ILLEGAL.

Look at the Venn diagram. Write the number of the paragraph that the detail fits into.

Paragraph 1: Lucas and Zoe are alike.

Paragraph 2: Lucas and Zoe are different.

_____ Lucas is afraid, but Zoe is not.

_____ They are skating in a competition.

_____ Zoe is good at reading, but Lucas has a hard time.

_____ They are brother and sister.

_____ Lucas has to try hard, but Zoe makes things look easy.

_____ Zoe cheers Lucas, but Lucas can't watch Zoe skate without getting scared.

✔ **Paragraph 1 should have details that explain how Lucas and Zoe are alike. Paragraph 2 should have details that explain how Lucas and Zoe are not alike. Here are the correct answers:**

__2__ Lucas is afraid, but Zoe is not.

__1__ They are skating in a competition.

__2__ Zoe is good at reading, but Lucas has a hard time.

__1__ They are brother and sister.

__2__ Lucas has to try hard, but Zoe makes things look easy.

__2__ Zoe cheers Lucas, but Lucas can't watch Zoe skate without getting scared.

Eric is now ready to write his draft.

© The Continental Press, Inc.   DUPLICATING THIS MATERIAL IS ILLEGAL.

Step 2: Drafting

Lucas and Zoe are alike sometimes. They are brother and sisters. Lucas can skate. Zoe skates good. They both skate in shows.

Zoe does everything right. She is never afraid. She win medals. Lucas is different. He is scared. He can't read very well. Zoe can. He can't watch Zoe skate. It makes him nervous. She cheers him on. He don't want to be scared. Maybe he'll win a medal.

What is the topic sentence in paragraph 1?

A Lucas and Zoe are alike sometimes.

B They are brother and sisters.

C Lucas can skate.

D Zoe skates good.

The topic sentence tells the main idea. Choice A is the correct answer. It tells that the main idea of paragraph 1 is how Lucas and Zoe are the same. Choices B, C, and D give details that support this main idea. They are incorrect.

© The Continental Press, Inc.   DUPLICATING THIS MATERIAL IS ILLEGAL.

What is the topic sentence in paragraph 2?

A Zoe does everything right.

B She is never afraid.

C Lucas is different.

D Maybe he'll win a medal.

> Choice C is the topic sentence. The main idea is that Lucas and Zoe are not alike. The topic sentence does not have to be the first sentence in a paragraph. Choices A, B, and D are incorrect.

What connecting words did Eric use?

_____

_____

_____

> Connecting words give clues. They tell which things are alike and which things are different. Here is a sample answer:

The connecting words and, both, and alike tell that two things are alike. The connecting word different tells how two things are not alike.

Eric's next step is to revise his paragraphs.

© The Continental Press, Inc.   DUPLICATING THIS MATERIAL IS ILLEGAL.

Step 3: Revising

Lucas and Zoe are alike ~~sometimes.~~ *in some ways.* They are brother and sisters. ~~Lucas can skate. Zoe skates good.~~ *They both skate.* They both ~~skate~~ *also compete* in shows.

But Zoe and Lucas are different, too. Zoe does everything right. She is never afraid. She win medals. Lucas is different. He is scared. He can't read very well. Zoe can. ~~He~~ *But Lucas* can't watch Zoe skate. It makes him nervous. She cheers him on. He don't want to be scared. ~~Maybe he'll win a medal.~~

Which sentences did Eric put together?

_____

_____

One way to revise your writing is to put together sentences that say the same thing. Here is a sample answer:

Eric put sentence 3 and sentence 4 together in the first paragraph to say, "They both skate."

© The Continental Press, Inc.   DUPLICATING THIS MATERIAL IS ILLEGAL.

What did Eric take out?

_____

_____

 A paragraph should have details that support the main idea. Sometimes, the sentence gives unimportant details. This means the sentence is not needed. Here is a sample answer:

Eric took out a sentence at the end that did not belong.

What connecting words did Eric add?

_____

_____

 Connecting words are clues that two things are the same. Or, they can be clues that two things are not the same. Here is a sample answer:

He added also, too, and but.

Peer Review

Eric used the checklist to review his writing. Then he exchanged papers with another student. They reviewed each other's writing and gave it a score based on the rubric. Then they discussed ways they could each improve their writing.

© The Continental Press, Inc.   DUPLICATING THIS MATERIAL IS ILLEGAL.

Checklist for Writing Alike and Different

Score 3
- The writing answers all parts of the question.
- The writing shows two ways the subjects are alike.
- The writing shows two ways the subjects are different.
- The writer uses connecting words.
- There are many good supporting details.
- Capitalization and punctuation are correct.

Score 2
- The writing answers almost all parts of the question.
- The writing shows one way the subjects are alike.
- The writing shows one way the subjects are different.
- The writer uses some connecting words.
- There are some supporting details.
- There are some mistakes in capitalization and punctuation.

Score 1
- The writing answers only part of the question.
- The writing does not show ways the subjects are alike.
- The writing does not show ways the subjects are different.
- The writer uses few or no connecting words.
- There are not many supporting details.
- There are many mistakes in capitalization and punctuation.

© The Continental Press, Inc.   DUPLICATING THIS MATERIAL IS ILLEGAL.

Step 4: Editing

Read the revised draft again. Find and correct three more mistakes.

Mistake 1: _____

Mistake 2: _____

Mistake 3: _____

Did you see any words that were not spelled correctly? Is correct punctuation used? These are the types of mistakes to look for when you edit your work. Here is the correct answer:

Mistake 1: Change sisters to sister in sentence 2.

Mistake 2: Change win to wins in sentence 8.

Mistake 3: Change don't to doesn't in sentence 16.

Step 5: Publishing

Eric published his paper by turning in his paper to his teacher.

© The Continental Press, Inc.   DUPLICATING THIS MATERIAL IS ILLEGAL.

Hazel Hutchins, Author

Hazel Hutchins is a popular children's book writer. She grew up in Canada, on the prairie. She loved books when she was a child. When she was 10 years old, she decided to be a writer. She loves to write stories about children. Her stories are very funny. Hazel Hutchins enjoys helping children write, too. She tells them about the way she writes. The Sidewalk Rescue is her 17th book with Ruth Ohi. She lives in Western Canada. She has three children.

Ruth Ohi, Illustrator

Ruth Ohi draws pictures for children's books. She started by collecting books. She wanted to be an artist. First, she worked with computers. Later, she decided to draw with chalk. Ruth's drawings are funny. She likes to draw pictures for humorous stories. She has also written a few children's books. Ruth gives talks to schoolchildren. She tells them about drawing. She enjoys helping children write and draw. The Sidewalk Rescue is her 17th book with Hazel Hutchins. Ruth Ohi lives in Eastern Canada. She has two children.

© The Continental Press, Inc.   DUPLICATING THIS MATERIAL IS ILLEGAL.

Hazel Hutchins is a writer. Ruth Ohi is an artist. They have worked together on many books. Read the paragraphs about these two people. Write two paragraphs about them. One paragraph should show how they are alike. One paragraph should show how they are different. Be sure to:

- tell at least two ways that they are alike
- tell at least two ways that they are different
- use details from the paragraphs to support your answer

1 What kind of writing are you being asked to do?

Read
Note
Organize

_____

_____

_____

_____

_____

2 Will your answer be written as two sentences or two paragraphs?

_____

_____

_____

_____

© The Continental Press, Inc.　DUPLICATING THIS MATERIAL IS ILLEGAL.

3 Fill in the circles in the Venn diagram. Use details from your reading. This will help you see what is the same and what is different.

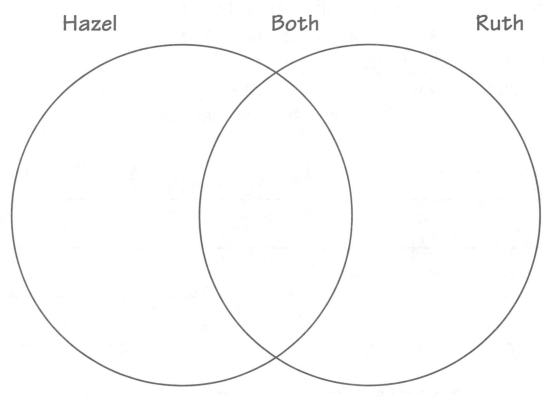

Hazel   Both   Ruth

What will you put in each paragraph? List ideas from your Venn diagram.

Paragraph 1: _____

_____

_____

_____

Paragraph 2: _____

_____

_____

_____

© The Continental Press, Inc.   DUPLICATING THIS MATERIAL IS ILLEGAL.

4 Now, write your draft. Use your Venn diagram and paragraph plans to help you write. Be sure you start each paragraph with a topic sentence. In the first paragraph, write about how the two people are alike. In the second paragraph, write about how they are different. Remember to use connecting words. Words such as <u>and</u>, <u>alike</u>, <u>like</u>, and <u>also</u> can show how the people are the same. Words such as <u>but</u>, <u>different</u>, and <u>unlike</u> can show how the two people are different.

_____

_____

_____

_____

_____

_____

_____

_____

_____

_____

© The Continental Press, Inc.   DUPLICATING THIS MATERIAL IS ILLEGAL.

5 Read back over your draft. Make your changes on this page. Check your draft for mistakes. Use the checklist on page 81 to review your own writing. Ask a classmate to edit your work if your teacher tells you to do so.

_____

_____

_____

_____

_____

_____

_____

_____

_____

_____

_____

_____

© The Continental Press, Inc.   DUPLICATING THIS MATERIAL IS ILLEGAL.

6 Write your final answer below. Publish it by showing it to your teacher.

_____

_____

_____

_____

_____

_____

_____

_____

_____

_____

_____

_____

_____

© The Continental Press, Inc.   DUPLICATING THIS MATERIAL IS ILLEGAL.

Types of Writing

You use the same writing steps for all the writing that you do. However, the types of writing you do are different. You might write a story. Or, you might write to give someone facts and details about a subject. Writing a story is different than writing for information. This unit will review the different types of writing.

- **In Lesson 6,** you will write an opinion. You will use facts in your writing. These facts will help support your opinion. It will also persuade someone to agree with you.

- **Lesson 7** is about descriptive writing. In this type of writing, you describe something. You create a word picture of the scene for your readers.

- **In Lesson 8,** you'll write a narrative. A narrative is a story with a beginning, middle, and end. A story also has a setting.

- **Lesson 9** tells how to write for information. This is the type of writing you do in class and on tests.

© The Continental Press, Inc.   DUPLICATING THIS MATERIAL IS ILLEGAL.

Reasoned Writing

W.2.1, 5, 6

A **fact** is a true statement. It can be proved. An **opinion** is what you think or believe. It cannot be proved. Sometimes, you are asked to write an opinion. You use facts to back up your opinion.

You should know how to tell a fact from an opinion. There are clue words that can help. They tell you that a statement is an opinion.

nobody	everybody
best	worst
most	least
always	never
believe	feel
think	seem

Sometimes, you **write to persuade.** This means you want someone to think the way you do. You begin with a topic sentence. This gives your opinion. It tells what you want your reader to believe or do. Then you want to back up your opinion. You use facts, examples, and reasons to do this. The last sentence sums up your opinion.

© The Continental Press, Inc. DUPLICATING THIS MATERIAL IS ILLEGAL.

Port City Gets Its Very Own Bike Path

The children of Port City are very happy today. It is the opening day of a new bike path in the city. Both parents and children have waited a long time for a path.

Children in Port City had nowhere to ride their bikes. The city parks have plenty of grass and trees that are fine for playing ball and having picnics. Grass does not work well for riding bicycles. Walkers on sidewalks don't want bikers there. Riding on the streets is not safe.

A group of Port City parents got together to learn about bike paths. A bike path is a safe place for people to ride. There is no traffic. The parents thought that the city should have a bike path. The path would connect schools, bus stops, and parks. Some people could bike to work. Then, there would be less traffic on the streets. Children could use the bike path to ride their bikes to school.

The parent group made a plan and sent it to the mayor. The mayor told them that the city did not have enough money to build the bike path, so people raised money for the project. Finally, the parent group got their wish. Now, children and adults have a safe place to ride their bikes.

© The Continental Press, Inc.   DUPLICATING THIS MATERIAL IS ILLEGAL.

Do you think your town or city should have more bike paths? Write a paragraph to people in your town to explain your opinion. Be sure to:

- write two or more reasons why you think this way
- use facts from the article to help you write

Step 1: Prewriting

Here is how one student, Marco, wrote his opinion. First, Marco read the question carefully. He read the question until he understood what he should do.

Read
Note
Organize

Then Marco made notes to himself. Here are the notes he made:

My subject—bike paths in my town
What I have to write—a paragraph
Who will read my writing—people in my town
What I have to do—write my opinion and two or more reasons for my opinion

Read
Note
Organize

Marco's next step was to think about what he believed. Should his town have a bike path? Do they need another bike path if there is already one?

Read
Note
Organize

© The Continental Press, Inc.   DUPLICATING THIS MATERIAL IS ILLEGAL.

First, Marco decided on an opinion. Next, he used a graphic organizer to help order his ideas. He wrote his opinion at the top. Then he wrote the reasons and facts for his opinion. Here is the organizer Marco used:

My Opinion: Clifton needs more bike paths.
Reason/Fact 1: We only have one bike path. It's very crowded on summer days. It goes too near the buses.
Reason/Fact 2: I want to ride my bike to school. Now, I have to ride in the street. It is not safe. Children can get hit by cars when they ride on city streets.
Reason/Fact 3:

What is another reason Marco can add to the chart?

_____

_____

Marco thinks there should be more bike paths. He needs to back up his opinion with a fact. Or, he needs to give a reason. Here is a sample answer:

People might stop using cars and use bikes instead.
There would be less traffic.

Marco is now ready to write his draft.

© The Continental Press, Inc.   DUPLICATING THIS MATERIAL IS ILLEGAL.

Step 2: Drafting

Clifton needs another bike path. We only have one. It is very crowed. On summer days, there is no room for children to ride. People ride on it too fast. they ride it to work. Also, the bike path is not close to the schools. if children want to ride their bikes to school, they have to ride on the road. I'm scared to ride on the road because I almost got hit once. Their are a lot of acidents! If we had another bike path, more people would use bikes. Some people might stop using cars. And there would be less traffic. People should ask the mayor. He should build Clifton a new bike path. It would be a good idea for everyone!

Which is the topic sentence in the paragraph?

A Clifton needs another bike path.

B We only have one.

C People ride on it too fast.

D Also, the bike path is not close to the schools.

 The topic sentence gives the main idea. Or, it states an opinion. Choice A tells Marco's opinion. This is the correct answer. Choices B, C, and D are incorrect. They are reasons that back up Marco's opinion.

© The Continental Press, Inc.   DUPLICATING THIS MATERIAL IS ILLEGAL.

How many facts or reasons does Marco use to support his opinion?

    A one

    B two

    C three

    D four

> ✓ Think about the graphic organizer Marco used. What reasons did he give for his opinion? Choice C is the correct answer. Choices A, B, and D are incorrect.

What is one of Marco's facts or reasons?

_____

_____

> ✓ How does Marco back up his opinion? Why does he think his town needs another bike path? Here is a sample answer:

There is only one path and it's too crowded.

Marco's next step is to revise his draft.

© The Continental Press, Inc.   DUPLICATING THIS MATERIAL IS ILLEGAL.

Step 3: Revising

Clifton needs another bike path. We only have one. It is very crow^d~ed~. On summer days, there is no room for children to ride. People ride (on it) too fast, ~they~ Lots of people ride it to work. Also, the bike path is not close to the schools. if children want to ride their bikes to school, they have to ride on the road. ~I'm scared to ride on the road because I almost got hit once.~ Their are a lot of acidents! If we had another bike path, more people would use bikes. Some people might stop using cars. ^And there would be less traffic. People should ask the mayor. ~He should~ to build Clifton a new bike path. It would be a good idea for everyone!

Why did Marco take out a sentence?

_____

_____

    Facts and reasons should back up an opinion. Sometimes, sentences are used that give facts that are not important. Or, they do not fit with the subject. Here is a sample answer:

Marco took out a sentence because it did not back up his opinion. It was not a strong reason.

© The Continental Press, Inc.   DUPLICATING THIS MATERIAL IS ILLEGAL.

Peer Review

Marco used this checklist to review his writing. Then he exchanged papers with another student. They reviewed each other's writing and gave it a score based on the rubric. Then they discussed ways they could improve their writing.

Checklist for Writing Opinions and Facts

Score 3
- The writing answers all parts of the question.
- The paragraph starts with a topic sentence that tells the writer's opinion.
- There are at least two good reasons for the opinion.
- Capitalization and punctuation are correct.

Score 2
- The writing answers almost all parts of the question.
- The topic sentence does not tell the writer's opinion.
- There is only one good reason for the opinion.
- There are some mistakes in capitalization and punctuation.

Score 1
- The writing answers only part of the question.
- There is no clear topic sentence.
- The reasons for the opinion are hard to understand.
- There are many mistakes in capitalization and punctuation.

Now, Marco is ready to edit his work.

© The Continental Press, Inc.   DUPLICATING THIS MATERIAL IS ILLEGAL.

Step 4: Editing

Read the revised draft on page 96 again. Find and correct three mistakes.

_____

_____

_____

 Mistakes need to be fixed in the editing stage. Look for misspelled words. Make sure the correct punctuation marks are used. Here are the correct answers:

Change if to If in sentence 8.

Change Their to There in sentence 9.

Change acidents to accidents in sentence 9.

Step 5: Publishing

The final step is for Marco to publish his writing. There are many ways to publish something. Marco could send his work to the town newspaper. He could send a letter. Or, he could make a poster explaining his opinion.

© The Continental Press, Inc.   DUPLICATING THIS MATERIAL IS ILLEGAL.

No More Floating Around

LAKETOWN, MD 7/8/11 The town pool in Laketown is usually full of children playing on their inner tubes and using water toys. After this weekend, floating toys and balls will not be allowed in the Laketown pool.

Many parents are happy about this decision. They say that the toys are unsafe and cause children to bump into each other. Little children find it hard to swim when big kids play ball in the pool. "Some children get a little rough with their toys," said Jo Fisher, a mother of three children. "It can be scary for the little ones."

Other parents don't agree. Mary Abbot says, "The children are used to water toys. They play with the same ones in the lake. The lifeguards should do their job and keep all the children safe. Also, some children need floating toys to stay in the deep end of the pool."

Louis Farmer, the director of the pool, said, "Young children who need water wings to stay afloat will still be able to use them. But larger toys, like inner tubes, are too bulky to use in the pool. And playing ball in the pool must stop. Too many children get hurt. Our biggest concern is the safety of our children."

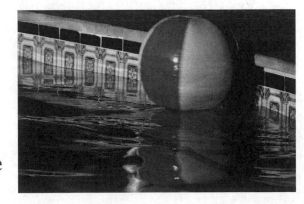

Not everyone agrees on this issue. But, now that there won't be water toys in the pool, there will be much more room to swim!

© The Continental Press, Inc.   DUPLICATING THIS MATERIAL IS ILLEGAL.

Some public swimming pools allow children to bring balls and other water toys. Others do not. What if children could not use water toys at your local swimming pool? Would you agree or disagree with that decision? Write a paragraph that gives your opinion. Be sure to:

- include a topic sentence to tell your opinion
- give at least two good reasons or facts for your opinion

1 What kind of writing are you being asked to do?

Read
Note
Organize

_____

_____

_____

_____

_____

© The Continental Press, Inc.   DUPLICATING THIS MATERIAL IS ILLEGAL.

2 What form will your writing be?

_____

_____

_____

_____

_____

3 Who will read your writing?

_____

_____

_____

_____

_____

© The Continental Press, Inc. **DUPLICATING THIS MATERIAL IS ILLEGAL.**

4 Fill in the opinion and reason chart below. This will help you answer the question.

Read
Note
Organize

My Opinion:
Reason/Fact 1:
Reason/Fact 2:
Reason/Fact 3:

© The Continental Press, Inc.   DUPLICATING THIS MATERIAL IS ILLEGAL.

5 Use your chart to help you as you write your draft. Be sure to begin your paragraph with a topic sentence. Make sure your topic sentence gives your opinion. Then write each reason for your opinion.

_____

_____

_____

_____

_____

_____

_____

_____

_____

_____

_____

_____

© The Continental Press, Inc.   DUPLICATING THIS MATERIAL IS ILLEGAL.

6 When you have finished your draft, go back over it. Make your changes on this page. Check your draft for any mistakes. Use the checklist on page 97 to review your writing. Have a classmate edit your writing if your teacher allows it.

_____

_____

_____

_____

_____

_____

_____

_____

_____

_____

_____

_____

© The Continental Press, Inc.   DUPLICATING THIS MATERIAL IS ILLEGAL.

7 Write your final copy on this page. Publish it by showing it to your teacher.

_____

_____

_____

_____

_____

_____

_____

_____

_____

_____

_____

_____

_____

© The Continental Press, Inc.   DUPLICATING THIS MATERIAL IS ILLEGAL.

Descriptive Writing

W.2.2, 5, 6, 8

Sometimes, you use words to make a picture. This is called **descriptive writing**. You can paint a word picture with details about things you see, hear, smell, taste, and feel.

A descriptive paragraph needs a topic sentence. This introduces the subject. The details that follow help your readers picture what you describe. Your last sentence will tell the feeling you get about what you are describing.

Guided Practice

Read the question. Then write a response.

You have been asked to write a paragraph about having lunch at your school cafeteria. Use details to describe this place. Talk about what it looks like, sounds like, smells like, and feels like. Be sure to:

- use details that make readers feel as if they are in the cafeteria
- arrange your details in an order that makes sense

© The Continental Press, Inc.   **DUPLICATING THIS MATERIAL IS ILLEGAL.**

Step 1: Prewriting

What words give you clues about what you will be writing?

Read
Note
Organize

_____

_____

_____

_____

 How do you know what the subject is? How do you know what type of writing you will do? Look for key words that give clues. Here is a sample answer:

The words <u>write a paragraph</u> tell what I am writing.

The words <u>lunch at your school cafeteria</u> tell the subject.

The words <u>describe this place</u> tell that I am writing a description.

© The Continental Press, Inc.   DUPLICATING THIS MATERIAL IS ILLEGAL.

The next step is to plan what you will write and how you will write it. Charts and webs can help you put your ideas in order.

What type of graphic organizer would you use?

Read
Note
Organize

A cause-and-effect chart

B five senses web

C Venn diagram

D compare-and-contrast chart

A cause-and-effect chart tells what happened and why. A Venn diagram and a compare-and-contrast chart are used to compare how two things are alike and contrast how they are different. Choices A, C, and D are incorrect. A five senses web helps organize what you hear, see, smell, taste, and feel. Choice B is the correct answer.

© The Continental Press, Inc.   DUPLICATING THIS MATERIAL IS ILLEGAL.

Here is how one student, Razenne, used a senses web. The question asked her to describe a place. She needs to use details about how the place looks, sounds, smells, and feels.

Subject: Lunch At My School Cafeteria
Sights lots of long tables lines of students waiting for lunch trays and the food counter
Sounds you hear students talking
Smells it smells like canned green beans all the time
Tastes the food is always mushy it is not very hot
Touch the plastic trays are hot from being washed
Thoughts/Feelings I like eating with my friends the food is bad

© The Continental Press, Inc.   DUPLICATING THIS MATERIAL IS ILLEGAL.

Read each detail. Each detail goes with a sense. Label each item with the correct sense. Use the word **sight, sound, smell, taste, touch,** or **feelings.**

_____ The lights in the room are very bright.

_____ The doors slam shut with a bang.

_____ The hamburgers taste like dust.

_____ I can smell the French fries cooking.

_____ It's fun to trade lunches with my friends.

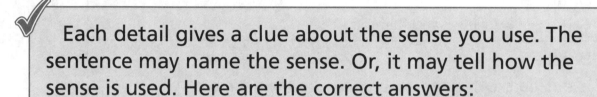

Each detail gives a clue about the sense you use. The sentence may name the sense. Or, it may tell how the sense is used. Here are the correct answers:

___sight__ The lights in the room are very bright.

__sound__ The doors slam shut with a bang.

__taste__ The hamburgers taste like dust.

__smell__ I can smell the French fries cooking.

feelings It's fun to trade lunches with my friends.

© The Continental Press, Inc.   DUPLICATING THIS MATERIAL IS ILLEGAL.

Step 2: Drafting

I eat lunch every day at my school. In the cafeteria it
is a big room there are lots of long tables. We all line up
we take trays. The trays feel really hot from the dishwashr.
I like the way my mom and dad cook. It is noise there
because everyone is talking all the time. the cafeteria
always smells green beens cooking all the time. The food is
mushy. It is not hot very much. I like eating with my
freinds but the food in my school does not taste great.

Why did Razenne leave a space at the beginning of her
paragraph?

_____

_____

  Think about a story you have read. How do you know
where one paragraph ends and the next one begins?
Here is a sample answer:

Razenne left a space to show the start of the paragraph.

© The Continental Press, Inc. DUPLICATING THIS MATERIAL IS ILLEGAL.

List three details Razenne gives about the cafeteria.

_____

_____

_____

✓ Can you picture the cafeteria? Razenne told what she saw, heard, smelled, and tasted during her lunch. How did she tell about these senses? Here is a sample answer:

lines of students waiting for lunch

it's noisy

the food is not very hot

What is the last point that Razenne makes about the cafeteria?

_____

_____

✓ The last sentence usually sums up the point of the paragraph. What does Razenne say about eating lunch in the cafeteria? Here is a sample answer:

Razenne likes eating with her friends, but the food does not taste that good.

Razenne is now ready to revise what she has written.

© The Continental Press, Inc.   DUPLICATING THIS MATERIAL IS ILLEGAL.

Step 3: Revising

Read Razenne's revised draft. Then answer the questions.

I eat lunch every day at my school. ~~If~~ the cafeteria ~~it~~
to get our food. Then
is a big room there are lots of long tables. We all line up
we take trays. The trays feel ~~really~~ hot from the dishwash*e*r.

~~I like the way my mom and dad cook.~~ It is nois*y* there

because everyone is talking all the time. the cafeteria

always smells *like* green beens cooking ~~all the time.~~ The food is

mushy. *and* ~~It~~ is not hot very much. I like eating with my

cafeteria
freinds but the food in my school does not taste great.

What sentence did Razenne cross out?

_____

_____

 Sometimes, a writer will take out words. She may also take out a sentence. The writer wants the words and sentences to back up the main idea. Those that do not are taken out. Here is a sample answer:

Razenne crossed out "I like the way my mom and dad cook."

© The Continental Press, Inc.   DUPLICATING THIS MATERIAL IS ILLEGAL.

Razenne switched the order of two words. What are the two words?

A mushy, and

B hot, very

C school, cafeteria

D smells, like

 Choice B is the correct answer. The sentence read <u>hot very</u>. Razenne changed the order of the words to now read <u>very hot</u>. Choices A, C, and D are incorrect. The words <u>and</u>, <u>cafeteria</u>, and <u>like</u> were added to sentences.

Peer Review

Razenne used the checklist to review her writing. Then she exchanged papers with another student. They reviewed each other's writing and gave it a score based on the rubric. Then they discussed ways they could improve their writing.

© The Continental Press, Inc. DUPLICATING THIS MATERIAL IS ILLEGAL.

Checklist for Writing to Describe

Score 3
- The writing answers all parts of the question.
- The details use words related to the five senses.
- The last sentence gives a clear feeling about the subject.
- Words are used correctly and well.
- Capitalization and punctuation are correct.

Score 2
- The writing answers almost all parts of the question.
- Some of the details use words related to the five senses.
- The last sentence gives some feeling about the subject.
- Some words are misused.
- There are some mistakes in capitalization and punctuation.

Score 1
- The writing answers only part of the question.
- The details don't use words related to the five senses.
- The last sentence does not give a clear feeling about the subject.
- Many words are overused or misused.
- There are many mistakes in capitalization and punctuation.

The next step is for Razenne to edit her paper.

© The Continental Press, Inc. DUPLICATING THIS MATERIAL IS ILLEGAL.

Step 4: Editing

Reread Razenne's revised draft on page 113. Then find and correct four more mistakes.

_____

_____

_____

_____

 Did you find all the mistakes? Are all the words spelled correctly? Are the correct punctuation marks used? Here are the correct answers:

Change there to There in sentence 3.

Change the to The in sentence 8.

Change beens to beans in sentence 8.

Change freinds to friends in the last sentence.

The last step is for Razenne to publish her work.

Step 5: Publishing

Razenne is ready to share her work. She can do this by turning in her work to the teacher. She can handwrite her paragraph. Or, she can use a computer to write her paragraph.

© The Continental Press, Inc. DUPLICATING THIS MATERIAL IS ILLEGAL.

Walking in the Woods

The woods are cool and quiet today—
The perfect place to rest or play
Or build a fort to hide away

I hear the birds call out their names—
the chickadees are playing games
and mockingbirds all do the same

The air smells green, all leaves and grass—
Dewdrops hang, clear as glass
From flowers huddled in a mass

And squirrels scramble to and fro—
Chasing each other high and low,
They seem to know just where to go

If I could jump from tree to tree,
I'd be like them, wild and free
Still, walking in the woods, I'm glad I'm me.

© The Continental Press, Inc.   DUPLICATING THIS MATERIAL IS ILLEGAL.

Think about the woods that are described in this poem. Write a paragraph describing a walk in these woods. Use details from the poem to help you write. Be sure to:

- describe the details using words about the five senses (sight, sound, smell, taste, and touch)
- write a topic sentence that tells the subject
- write a last sentence that tells how you feel about the subject

1 What kind of writing are you being asked to do? How do you know?

Read
Note
Organize

_____

_____

_____

_____

_____

2 What subject is the question asking you to write about?

_____

_____

_____

_____

_____

UNIT 2
Types of Writing

© The Continental Press, Inc.   DUPLICATING THIS MATERIAL IS ILLEGAL.

3 Use this chart to help plan your answer to the question.

Subject: Walk in the Woods
Sights
Sounds
Smells
Tastes
Touch
Thoughts/Feelings

© The Continental Press, Inc.   DUPLICATING THIS MATERIAL IS ILLEGAL.

4 Now, it's your turn to write a draft. First, look at your chart. Think about how your topic sentence talks about the subject. Think about the details that support the subject. Do the details make the reader feel like they are there? Make sure to use interesting words.

_____

_____

_____

_____

_____

_____

_____

_____

_____

_____

_____

_____

© The Continental Press, Inc.   DUPLICATING THIS MATERIAL IS ILLEGAL.

5 When you have finished your draft, go back over it. Make your changes on this page. Edit your draft. Use the checklist on page 115 to review the paper. Ask a classmate to review it if the teacher tells you to do so.

_____

_____

_____

_____

_____

_____

_____

_____

_____

_____

_____

© The Continental Press, Inc.   DUPLICATING THIS MATERIAL IS ILLEGAL.

6 Write your final answer on this page. Then publish
your work by showing it to your teacher.

_____

_____

_____

_____

_____

_____

_____

_____

_____

_____

_____

_____

_____

_____

© The Continental Press, Inc. DUPLICATING THIS MATERIAL IS ILLEGAL.

Narrative Writing

W.2.3, 5, 6, 8

When you write a story, you need a clear beginning, middle, and end. You might write a story about the first time you took a field trip. Or, you might make up a story. When you write about yourself, you use the pronouns I and me.

You write the details in a story in the order that they happened. You should also choose a place and time for your story. This is called the **setting.** The time might be "yesterday." The place could be your classroom.

Guided Practice

Read the question. Then answer the questions and write a response.

Write a story about the first time you lost a tooth. Be sure to:

- write details about the event
- write your details in the order they happened
- write a paragraph

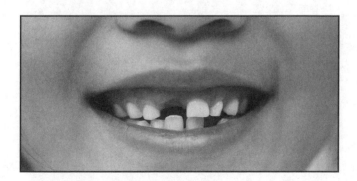

© The Continental Press, Inc.   DUPLICATING THIS MATERIAL IS ILLEGAL.

Step 1: Prewriting

Here is how one student, Terrelle, answered the question. First, Terrelle read the question carefully. The words <u>about the first time you lost a tooth</u> told him he would be writing a story about losing his first tooth.

Read
Note
Organize

Then he read the question again. He looked for clues about how to tell his story. The words <u>in the order they happened</u> let him know he should use time order.

Read
Note
Organize

Who is your audience?

A parents

B classmates

C friends

D teacher

The question does not say who the audience is. However, you can guess that it is a teacher. A teacher often asks you to write a story. Choice D is the correct answer. Choices A, B, and C are incorrect.

© The Continental Press, Inc.   DUPLICATING THIS MATERIAL IS ILLEGAL.

The next step is to plan what you will write. A graphic organizer can help you write down your ideas. This question asked Terrelle to write a story about an event in his life. He chose a chart to help him write down the details of his story in time order.

Subject: How I Lost My First Tooth	
1	I was 5 years old.
2	All my friends lost a tooth already.
3	One of my bottom front teeth started to wiggle.
4	I was afraid all my teeth would fall out.
5	
6	
7	

© The Continental Press, Inc.   DUPLICATING THIS MATERIAL IS ILLEGAL.

What do you think happened next? Number the sentences 5, 6, or 7 in the time order you think they happened.

_____ I showed my mother the wiggly tooth.

_____ I got a dollar in a tooth-fairy box on my dresser.

_____ My mother had to pull it out. She didn't want me to swallow it.

> ✓ **Think about how an event caused something to happen. This will help you determine the order of events in the story. Here is the correct answer:**

_5_ I showed my mother the wiggly tooth.

_7_ I got a dollar in a tooth-fairy box on my dresser.

_6_ My mother had to pull it out. She didn't want me to swallow it.

© The Continental Press, Inc.   DUPLICATING THIS MATERIAL IS ILLEGAL.

Step 2: Drafting

I lost my first tooth when was 5 years old. All my friends lost a tooth alredy and I though I never lose one. One of my bottem front teeth started to wiggle I was afraid all my teeth woud fall out and I couldnt eat anything. It felt weird I was really scared. So I showed my mother the wigly tooth. But it didnt fall out it took two whole months. My mother didn't want me to swallow my tooth so she pulled it. It hurt a little and it bled. But I was fine. I put the tooth in a tooth-fairy box on my dresser. I got a dollar the next morning in the box. I couldn't wait for the next tooth to come out!

What is the main idea of Terrelle's story?

_____

_____

 Look for the topic sentence. This tells the main idea of the story. Here is a sample answer:

Terrelle's story is about losing his first tooth.

© The Continental Press, Inc.   DUPLICATING THIS MATERIAL IS ILLEGAL.

What words did Terrelle use to show the time order of the details in his story?

_____

_____

 How do you know the order of events? Terrelle used clue words that tell when something happened. Here is the correct answer:

first tooth, when, so, two whole months, the next morning, next tooth

Terrelle is now ready to revise his draft.

© The Continental Press, Inc.   DUPLICATING THIS MATERIAL IS ILLEGAL.

Step 3: Revising

I lost my first tooth when was 5 years old. All my

friends lost a tooth alredy and I though I never lose one.
t *would*

One day,
Øne of my bottem front teeth started to wiggle I was

afraid all my teeth woud fall out and I couldnt eat

anything. It felt weird I was really scared. So I showed my

mother the wigly tooth. But it didnt fall out it took two

whole months. My mother didn't want me to swallow my

tooth so she pulled it. It hurt a little and it bled. But I

was fine. I put the tooth in a tooth-fairy box on my

dresser. I got a dollar the next morning in the box. I

couldn't wait for the next tooth to come out!

Why did Terrelle add the words <u>One day</u>?

_____

_____

Think about what you learn from the words <u>One day</u>.
Do they describe something? Do they give a cause or
effect? Do they indicate when something happened?
Here is a sample answer:

Terrelle added <u>One day</u> to show the time order of the
detail in that sentence.

© The Continental Press, Inc.   DUPLICATING THIS MATERIAL IS ILLEGAL.

Why did Terrelle add the word <u>would</u> to sentence 2?

_____

_____

 A complete sentence must have a subject and a verb. Verbs can also tell when an action happened. Here is a sample answer:

Terrelle added <u>would</u> to make a complete sentence.

Peer Review

The next step is to have a classmate check your writing. Terrelle used a checklist to review his writing. Then he exchanged papers with another student. They reviewed each other's writing and gave it a score based on the rubric. Then they discussed ways they could improve their writing.

© The Continental Press, Inc.   DUPLICATING THIS MATERIAL IS ILLEGAL.

Checklist for Writing a Story

Score 3
- The writing answers all parts of the question.
- There is a clear beginning, middle, and end to the story.
- Details are interesting and are in a sensible order.
- The place and time of the story are clear.
- Capitalization and punctuation are correct.

Score 2
- The writing answers almost all parts of the question.
- Parts of the beginning, middle, or end to the story are not clear.
- Not all details are in order or make sense.
- The place and time of the story are not clear.
- There are some mistakes in capitalization and punctuation.

Score 1
- The writing answers only part of the question.
- There is not a clear beginning, middle, or end to the story.
- Many details are missing or the order is unclear.
- The writer doesn't describe the place or time of the story.
- There are many mistakes in capitalization and punctuation

Terrelle's next step is to edit his paper.

© The Continental Press, Inc.   DUPLICATING THIS MATERIAL IS ILLEGAL.

Step 4: Editing

Find and correct five more mistakes in Terrelle's draft.

_____

_____

Look for words that are misspelled. Make sure that every complete sentence has a punctuation mark. Check that punctuation is used the right way. Here are the correct answers:

Add the pronoun I before was in sentence 1.
Change alredy to already in sentence 2.
Change bottem to bottom in sentence 3.
Change wigly to wiggly in sentence 7.
Change didnt to didn't in sentence 8.

The next step is for Terrelle to publish his work.

Step 5: Publishing

There are many ways to publish a story. Terrelle can use a computer to write his story. Then he can turn in his story to his teacher. Or, he can read it to the class. He can even enter it into a contest.

© The Continental Press, Inc.   DUPLICATING THIS MATERIAL IS ILLEGAL.

Dominic Gets a Pet

Dominic always wanted a pet. He asked for a cat. His mother said, "No, Dominic, you know we can't have cats in this apartment." He asked for a mouse. His mother said, "Absolutely not. I've told you before, Dominic. We can't have animals in this apartment." But most of all, Dominic wanted a dog. He begged and pleaded, but his mother would hear none of it. It seemed that Dominic would never have a pet.

One day—a day that seemed like any other day—Dominic came home from school. He rushed up the five flights of stairs to the apartment, like he always did. He started to toss his bag on the kitchen table. But there was something already sitting on the kitchen table. Something that was staring at him through a large glass bowl. Something gold and wiggly with a funny little mouth and huge eyes . . . Dominic gasped. He could hardly breathe, he was so excited! It was a fish!

Dominic ran into the family room. He tackled his mother with the biggest hug he could give her. "I thought we couldn't have pets, Mama!" Dominic squealed. "We can't have pets with fur and feet," she replied, a smile spreading on her face. "What will you name your new friend, Dom?" Dominic thought for a moment. "I'll call him Fido!" Dominic and his mother both laughed. What a perfect name for his first pet!

© The Continental Press, Inc.   DUPLICATING THIS MATERIAL IS ILLEGAL.

Pretend that you are Dominic's best friend. Write a one-paragraph story about the day you found out that Dominic had a new pet. In your story, be sure to:

- write events in the order they happened
- use details that make the story seem real
- write about the place and time of the story

Read
Note
Organize

1 What kind of writing are you being asked to do?

_____

_____

_____

_____

_____

2 Who will read your writing?

_____

_____

_____

_____

_____

© The Continental Press, Inc.   DUPLICATING THIS MATERIAL IS ILLEGAL.

3 Use this time order chart to plan your answer.

Subject:	
1	
2	
3	
4	
5	
6	
7	

© The Continental Press, Inc.   DUPLICATING THIS MATERIAL IS ILLEGAL.

4 Now, it is your turn to write a draft. First, look at your chart. Think about the main subject of your paragraph. Did you write the details in time order? Remember to use words that make your story interesting. Make readers want to know what happens next.

_____

_____

_____

_____

_____

_____

_____

_____

_____

_____

_____

_____

© The Continental Press, Inc.   DUPLICATING THIS MATERIAL IS ILLEGAL.

5 When you have finished your draft, go back over it. Make your changes on this page. Edit your draft. Use the checklist on page 131 to check your paper. Have a classmate edit your paragraph if your teacher says to do so.

_____

_____

_____

_____

_____

_____

_____

_____

_____

_____

_____

_____

© The Continental Press, Inc.   DUPLICATING THIS MATERIAL IS ILLEGAL.

6 Write your final copy on the lines below. Publish your work by showing it your teacher.

_____

_____

_____

_____

_____

_____

_____

_____

_____

_____

_____

_____

_____

_____

UNIT 2 ▪▪
Types of Writing

© The Continental Press, Inc.   DUPLICATING THIS MATERIAL IS ILLEGAL.

Informational Writing

W.2.2, 5, 6, 8

When you write a report, you tell facts or you explain something. You write to give **information.** You also may do this kind of writing when you answer a question.

You can set up your writing in a few ways. One way is by main idea and details. Another way is by cause and effect. A third way is to write steps in the right order.

Guided Practice

Read the assignment. Then answer the questions.

Tell someone who has moved next door to you how to borrow books from your town library. Be sure to:
- put the steps in order
- write all the steps you usually follow
- write one paragraph

© The Continental Press, Inc.   DUPLICATING THIS MATERIAL IS ILLEGAL.

Step 1: Prewriting

Here's how one student, Remy, began the assignment. First, he read the question carefully. He saw the words <u>tell</u> and <u>how to</u>. He was to tell how to do something. He saw the words <u>steps</u> and <u>order</u>. He would need to think about what you do first, next, and last to take a book from the library.

Read
Note
Organize

Who is the audience?

A a new principal

B a new teacher

C a new neighbor

D a new classmate

Remy read the question once more. He spotted "someone who has moved next door." Remy knew he would be writing for a new neighbor. Choice C is the correct answer. Choices A, B, and D are incorrect.

The next step is to plan what you will write. Use a chart to help you write down your ideas. This question asked Remy to write steps for borrowing a book from the library. He decided to use a step chart. This would help him put his thoughts in the right order.

Read
Note
Organize

How to Take a Book out of the Library
Step 1 First, you have to have a library card.
Step 2 Next, you pick which book you want.
Step 3 Then, you take your book to the checkout desk.
Step 4
Step 5

© The Continental Press, Inc.   DUPLICATING THIS MATERIAL IS ILLEGAL.

Choose two items that complete the step chart. Label
your choices Step 4 and Step 5.

_____ The librarian scans your library card and your book.

_____ The library has books on every subject.

_____ My librarian's name is Mrs. Ramos.

_____ You give the librarian your card and the book.

✓ Each cause has an effect. You can tell by the cause
and the effect the order that something happens. Think
about the causes and effects in these items. Here is a
sample answer:

Step 5 The librarian scans your library card and your book.

_____ The library has books on every subject.

_____ My librarian's name is Mrs. Ramos.

Step 4 You give the librarian your card and the book.

Remy finished his plan. He is ready to start writing.

© The Continental Press, Inc.   DUPLICATING THIS MATERIAL IS ILLEGAL.

Step 2: Drafting

It's easy if you want to check out a book from the libary. First, you have to tell the librarian that you would like to get a libary card. You pick out the book you want. Then you bring the book to the librarian at the chekout desk. This is when you give her your card. My librarian's name is Mrs. Ramos. Next, the librarian takes your card and book and scans them. and gives you a paper with the date it is due. Remember to return the book by the due date. If you don't, I will pay a find. Now, that's all you have to do take out a book from the libary!

What is the main idea of Remy's draft?

_____

_____

 Look for Remy's topic sentence. This gives the main idea. It tells Remy's purpose in writing. Here is a sample answer:

The main idea is how to take out a library book.

© The Continental Press, Inc. DUPLICATING THIS MATERIAL IS ILLEGAL.

What connecting words did Remy use to show the order?

_____

_____

> ✓ Some words give clues about order. They tell when something should happen. Many how-to paragraphs have words that tell the order. Here's a sample answer:

Remy used the connecting words First, Then, Next, and Now.

Why does Remy's last sentence work well?

_____

_____

> ✓ The last sentence should sum up the paragraph. Here is a sample answer:

It lets the reader know there are no more steps to follow.

Next, Remy will revise his writing.

© The Continental Press, Inc.   DUPLICATING THIS MATERIAL IS ILLEGAL.

Step 3: Revising

It's easy ~~if you want~~ to check out a book from the

li^rbary. First, you have to tell the librarian that you would

After you get your card,

like to get a li^rbary card. You pick out the book you want.

Then you bring the book to the librarian at the chekout

desk. This is when you give her your card. ~~My librarian's~~

~~name is Mrs. Ramos.~~ Next, the librarian takes your card and

Then she

book and scans them. ~~and~~ gives you a paper with the date

it is due. Remember to return the book by the due date. If

you

you don't, ^I will pay a find. Now, that's all you have to do

take out a book from the libary!

Why did Remy cross out the sentence about Mrs. Ramos?

_____

_____

 Think about what you learned about main idea and details. The details in a paragraph must support the main idea. Here is a sample answer:

Remy took it out because it was not a step explaining how to check out a book.

© The Continental Press, Inc.   DUPLICATING THIS MATERIAL IS ILLEGAL.

Peer Review

Remy used this checklist to review his writing. Then he exchanged papers with another student. They reviewed each other's writing and gave it a score based on the rubric. Then they discussed ways they could improve their writing.

Checklist for Writing to Give Information

Score 3

- The writing answers all parts of the question.
- The topic sentence tells a main idea.
- Details support the main idea.
- The writing uses many connecting words.
- Capitalization and punctuation are correct.

Score 2

- The writing answers almost all parts of the question.
- There is a main idea.
- Some details support the main idea.
- The writing uses some connecting words.
- There are some mistakes in capitalization and punctuation.

Score 1

- The writing answers only part of the question.
- The main idea is unclear.
- Few details support the main idea.
- The writing does not use connecting words.
- There are many mistakes in capitalization and punctuation.

Now, Remy can edit his paper.

© The Continental Press, Inc.   DUPLICATING THIS MATERIAL IS ILLEGAL.

Step 4: Editing

Proofread Remy's revised draft on page 144. Find and correct four more mistakes.

_____

_____

_____

_____

 Are there any words that are spelled wrong? Is all the punctuation used correctly? These are some mistakes to look for when editing. Here are the correct answers:

Change You to you in sentence 3.
Change chekout to checkout in sentence 4.
Change find to fine in sentence 9.
Change libary to library in the last sentence.

Step 5: Publishing

The last step is to publish your writing. Remy can give the paragraph to his new neighbor. He can also ask the librarian if she wants him to make a poster of the steps. She can then display it in the library.

© The Continental Press, Inc.   DUPLICATING THIS MATERIAL IS ILLEGAL.

Exploring Mars: Today We Know More About the Red Planet

Mars is the fourth planet from the sun. It has been nicknamed the Red Planet. The soil on Mars is a red color, and the sky is a pinkish red. For a long time, people thought that there might be life on Mars. From far away, it looked like Mars had seasons just like Earth. That's why people thought that Mars might have some kind of life on it.

We have learned much more about Mars from space exploration. In 1964, a space shuttle sent back 22 pictures from Mars. The pictures showed that the surface of Mars was nothing but rocks and soil. The planet was marked with craters and natural channels. Tests showed that the air on Mars had hardly any oxygen. The temperature was very cold. There were no signs of life on Mars.

The new Rover mission showed us more about Mars. Now, we know that there was water on Mars a long time ago. There may even have been floods there! We also know more about what the soil is made of. There are still no signs of life on Mars. But we know that Mars once had the water and kind of soil that living things need. Scientists are still exploring Mars. They want to learn more about what Mars was like long ago. Scientists believe that there are exciting things to discover about Mars.

© The Continental Press, Inc.   DUPLICATING THIS MATERIAL IS ILLEGAL.

Write one or more paragraphs that tell about Mars. First, tell what people thought about Mars before we explored space. Then tell about what we now know. Use details from the article. Be sure to:
- have a topic sentence and main idea
- use connecting words like <u>first</u>, <u>next</u>, and <u>last</u>

Read
Note
Organize

1 What kind of writing are you being asked to do?

_____

_____

_____

_____

_____

2 Who will read your writing?

_____

_____

_____

_____

_____

© The Continental Press, Inc.   DUPLICATING THIS MATERIAL IS ILLEGAL.

3 Use this chart to plan your answer.

Main idea:
What we knew before
What we know now

© The Continental Press, Inc.   DUPLICATING THIS MATERIAL IS ILLEGAL.

4 Now, it is your turn to write a draft. Before you begin, look at your chart. Think about your topic sentence. What should it be? What will you explain? Are all the facts and events in order? Do you need to add details? Remember to use connecting words such as <u>first</u>, <u>next</u>, <u>after</u>, and <u>last</u>.

_____

_____

_____

_____

_____

_____

_____

_____

_____

_____

_____

_____

© The Continental Press, Inc.   DUPLICATING THIS MATERIAL IS ILLEGAL.

5 When you have finished your draft, go back over it. Make your changes on this page. Edit your draft. Use the checklist on page 145 to check your work. Have a classmate check your work if your teacher says to do so.

_____

_____

_____

_____

_____

_____

_____

_____

_____

_____

_____

_____

© The Continental Press, Inc.   DUPLICATING THIS MATERIAL IS ILLEGAL.

6 Write your final copy on this page. Publish your work by showing it to your teacher.

_____

_____

_____

_____

_____

_____

_____

_____

_____

_____

_____

_____

_____

_____

© The Continental Press, Inc.   DUPLICATING THIS MATERIAL IS ILLEGAL.

Research

You know how to write for a test. You also know how to write for the classroom. This unit looks at a different kind of writing. The research paper is a report. You will learn how to find facts. Then you will learn how to organize them.

- **Lesson 10** tells how to find a topic. It also tells how to find facts.

- **In Lesson 11,** you'll learn how to write a strong thesis statement. You'll also learn how to sort your facts. An outline will help you do this.

- **Lesson 12** is about how to write a research paper. This lesson will help you create a source list. It will also help you pick visual aids for your paper.

© The Continental Press, Inc.   DUPLICATING THIS MATERIAL IS ILLEGAL.

Researching Sources and Content

W.2.2, 5–8

What if you want to find out more about your favorite author? Where would you look? This type of fact finding is called **researching.**

You might do research for a class project. Or, you might do it because you want to know more. Knowing where to find facts is an important skill.

After you find your information, you might be asked to share it. You can do this by writing a report. Writing a report is done in steps like the other writing you do.

Step 1: Pick a topic.

Step 2: Research the topic.

Step 3: Develop the thesis statement.

Step 4: Outline the paper.

Step 5: Write the paper.

Step 6: Tell the sources.

Step 1: Pick a Topic

Your teacher might give you a topic. Or, you might pick your own. A topic should be big enough to write about in a few pages. However, it should not be too big. If it is, you will need to write many, many pages about the topic. If it is too small, you won't be able to write enough to fill a few pages. You must narrow your topic.

© The Continental Press, Inc.   DUPLICATING THIS MATERIAL IS ILLEGAL.

Guided Practice

Read the questions. Then answer them.

Which of these would make the <u>best</u> topic for a paper?

    A famous places of the world

    B famous places of the United States

    C famous places of Philadelphia

    D famous places of Pennsylvania

A topic should be just right. It should not be so big that you write more than a few pages. It must not be so small that you cannot write a page or two about it. Choices A, B, and D are too broad. They are incorrect. The correct answer is choice C.

Which of these would make the <u>best</u> topic for a research paper?

    A the best cars

    B cars from the 1950s

    C cars built in Detroit

    D the Mustang convertible

A research paper should have a narrow topic. This makes it easier to research and write about it. Choice D is the narrowest topic. It is about one type of car. Choice D is the correct answer. Choices A, B, and C are too broad. They are incorrect.

© The Continental Press, Inc.   DUPLICATING THIS MATERIAL IS ILLEGAL.

Step 2: Research the Topic

The next step is to find facts about your topic. There are many ways to find information.

You can

- ask someone who knows about the subject.
- read a book about it.
- check a website.
- look in a reference book.

There are different kinds of reference books you can use.

Almanacs—These list interesting facts about subjects during a certain year.

Atlases—These show maps of countries, states, and regions.

Encyclopedias—These give information about all types of subjects.

Some parts of a book can also help you with your research. All books have a **table of contents.** It is at the front of the book. It lists the names of the chapters. It tells the page where each chapter begins. You can read the chapter names. They may have words related to the subject you are researching. Then you can check the chapter to see if there are any facts for your paper.

There are others parts of a book that can be helpful, too.

Title page lists the name of the book and the author. This is at the front of the book.

Copyright page tells when it was published and the publisher. It is on the back of the title page.

Glossary lists key words and their meanings. It is at the back of the book.

Index lists the subjects in a book in ABC order. It also says what page in the book tells about the subject. The index is at the back of the book.

© The Continental Press, Inc.　DUPLICATING THIS MATERIAL IS ILLEGAL.

Guided Practice

Read the table of contents. Then answer the questions.

All About Beavers
Table of Contents

Where in the book would you find facts about a beaver's habitat?

A Chapter 1

B Chapter 2

C Chapter 3

D Chapter 4

A habitat is where an animal lives. You would learn about a habitat in Chapter 3 "Where Beavers Live." Choice C is the correct answer. Choices A, B, and D are incorrect. These chapters give other facts about beavers.

© The Continental Press, Inc.   DUPLICATING THIS MATERIAL IS ILLEGAL.

Where in the book would you read about a beaver making a dam?

A Chapter 1

B Chapter 2

C Chapter 3

D Chapter 4

Making a dam is something that a beaver does. Chapter 2 would explain how a beaver makes a dam. Choice B is the correct answer. Choices A, C, and D are incorrect. These chapters give facts about what a beaver looks like, where it lives, and what it eats.

Knowing if the source can be trusted is important. Sometimes, information can be wrong. New discoveries might mean that the facts change. Or, the information might be an opinion. An opinion is not a fact. It is what someone thinks or believes.

A good researcher thinks like a detective. Here are some questions that will help you do this:

- What is the source of the information?
- How old is the information?
- Who wrote the information?
- Why did they write the information?
- Do other sources agree?

© The Continental Press, Inc.   DUPLICATING THIS MATERIAL IS ILLEGAL.

Notetaking

When you find your facts, you want to write them down. This makes it easier to write your paper. The best way to write down your facts is on a note card.

You can **summarize** what you have read. This is when you explain the main idea and important details. You can also **paraphrase.** This is when you use your own words to tell about a main idea.

Use a note card to take notes. Write the fact on the card. Then write where you found the fact. Here is how one student took notes.

Source {

<u>Seahorses</u>   Page 10

by Henry Davis   (Science Book Press, 2011)

Some seahorses are very small. They are the size of a fingernail.

} Fact

© The Continental Press, Inc.   DUPLICATING THIS MATERIAL IS ILLEGAL.

Guided Practice

Every state has symbols. The symbols show special things about the state. Most states have state flags and state songs. Many states also have state flowers and state animals.

New York's state flower is the rose. The rose was adopted as the state flower in 1955. Roses are fragrant with soft petals. The stems have sharp thorns.

The state insect is the ladybug. It is orange or red. It has black spots. Ladybugs are helpful in the garden. They eat tiny pests that feed on plants.

New York's state bird is the bluebird. It is one of the first birds to fly north each spring.

The beaver is the state animal. Early colonists traded beaver pelts. The fur traders settled near Albany. Albany is now the state capital.

New York's state symbols make New York special. Keep your eyes open. You may be lucky enough to spot one of these state treasures.

© The Continental Press, Inc.   DUPLICATING THIS MATERIAL IS ILLEGAL.

Which paragraph does <u>not</u> contain any facts that could
be included in a summary of the article?

A paragraph 2

B paragraph 3

C paragraph 5

D paragraph 6

Paragraphs 2, 3, and 5 all have main ideas that would
be in a summary of the article. Choices A, B, and C are
incorrect. Paragraph 6 just restates the topic sentence.
Choice D is the correct answer.

Paraphrase paragraph 3.

_____

_____

To paraphrase something means to put it into your own
words. Here is a sample answer:

New York's state insect is the ladybug. This insect is
red with black spots. You can find it in many gardens.

© The Continental Press, Inc.   DUPLICATING THIS MATERIAL IS ILLEGAL.

Test Yourself

1 Which of these would tell you what a key word meant?

   A index

   B table of contents

   C copyright

   D glossary

2 Which of these would be the <u>best</u> topic for a paper?

   A the 50 states

   B the Southern states

   C the Carolina states

   D North Carolina

3 Which of these would have only maps?

   A atlas

   B dictionary

   C almanac

   D encyclopedia

© The Continental Press, Inc.   DUPLICATING THIS MATERIAL IS ILLEGAL.

4 Where would you find information about seahorses?

A Chapter 1

B Chapter 2

C Chapter 3

D Chapter 4

5 What does it mean to paraphrase?

_____

_____

_____

_____

© The Continental Press, Inc. DUPLICATING THIS MATERIAL IS ILLEGAL.

Outlining the Research Paper

W.2.2, 5–8

The first step in writing a report is to pick a subject. The second step is to find out about the subject. The next step is to sort the information.

Step 3: Determine the Thesis Statement

You learned about the main idea in Lesson 3. The **thesis statement** is like the main idea. It tells the purpose of your paper.

The thesis statement is one sentence. It is in the first paragraph. A thesis statement is not a fact. It is a general statement that is supported by facts. It tells the reader what he will learn.

© The Continental Press, Inc. DUPLICATING THIS MATERIAL IS ILLEGAL.

Guided Practice

Answer the questions.

Which of these is the <u>best</u> thesis statement?

   A My report is about an important place.

   B Washington, D.C., was not the first capital of the United States.

   C New York City has many firsts, including the first capital of the new country.

   D New York was the capital of the United States until 1790.

   A thesis is not a fact. Choices B and D are incorrect. These are facts. Choice A is too general. Choice A is incorrect. The correct answer is choice C. This sums up the main idea of the paper.

Which of these is the <u>best</u> thesis statement?

   A Thomas Jefferson was our third president.

   B Thomas Jefferson wrote the Declaration of Independence.

   C Thomas Jefferson helped our new nation in many ways.

   D Thomas Jefferson created buildings.

   Choices A, B, and D are facts. They tell about Jefferson. These are incorrect. Choice C is the correct answer. Choices A, B, and D support the thesis statement.

© The Continental Press, Inc. DUPLICATING THIS MATERIAL IS ILLEGAL.

Step 4: Outline the Paper

The outline helps you plan your paper. It helps you sort your facts. First, write down the main ideas. Then give them a letter. Next, list details that support this idea. Number them. Now, you have sorted your facts into an outline. Here is an example of an outline.

```
   I.   Thesis statement

  II.   Body
        A. Main Idea
           1. Detail
           2. Detail

        B. Main Idea
           1. Detail
           2. Detail

        C. Main Idea
           1. Detail
           2. Detail

 III.   Conclusion
```

Each main idea will be a paragraph in your paper.

Sometimes, you find that you need more facts. You can look for more facts that support your main ideas. If you have too many facts about a main idea, you can use only the most important one. You do not have to use all your facts. You should use the details that best support your main ideas.

The **conclusion** is the sentence that sums up the purpose of the paper. It is in the last paragraph.

© The Continental Press, Inc. DUPLICATING THIS MATERIAL IS ILLEGAL.

Guided Practice

I.   Thesis statement: Thomas Jefferson created many important buildings.

II. Body
   A. _____
      1. Monticello
      2. Jefferson lived here with his family
   B. _____
      1. University of Virginia
      2. school for young people to learn
   C. _____
      1. Virginia State Capitol
      2. Virginia's government met here

Match each main idea below with the details that support it.

_____ built a government building

_____ built his house

_____ built a school

 The details support each main idea. These main ideas and details support the thesis statement. Here are the correct answers:

   _C_ built a government building

   _A_ built his house

   _B_ built a school

© The Continental Press, Inc.   DUPLICATING THIS MATERIAL IS ILLEGAL.

Test Yourself

1 Where should the thesis statement appear in a research paper?

    A in the beginning paragraph

    B in the middle paragraph

    C in the last paragraph

    D in the title

2 How does an outline help you write your paper?

_____

_____

_____

_____

3 Which is the <u>best</u> thesis statement?

    A Abraham Lincoln had his own holiday named Lincoln's Birthday.

    B George Washington had a holiday called Washington's Birthday.

    C Today, Presidents' Day honors both President Lincoln and President Washington.

    D Many of our national holidays were changed in the 1970s.

© The Continental Press, Inc.   DUPLICATING THIS MATERIAL IS ILLEGAL.

4 Read the outline. Where would you add these details in the outline below?

1. celebrate our freedom from England

1. remember people who died fighting for the America

1. remember the hard work of our laborers, or workers

```
  I.  Thesis: National holidays are ways to
      remember America's past every year.

 II.  Body
      A. Memorial Day

         1. _____
         2. speeches, parades, put flags on
            soldiers' graves
         3. was May 30, last Monday in May
            since 1970s

      B. Independence Day

         1. _____
         2. fireworks, parades
         3. July 4

      C. Labor Day

         1. _____
         2. fireworks
         3. first Monday in September

III.  Conclusion: The United States has
      national holidays to remember days
      and people that are important to
      America's history
```

© The Continental Press, Inc.   DUPLICATING THIS MATERIAL IS ILLEGAL.

Writing the Research Paper

W.2.2, 5–8

Writing a research paper is the same as other writing you do. You use the same steps. Once you have planned your report, then you are ready to write it.

Step 5: Write the Research Paper

You have already planned your paper. Now, you are ready to write your draft. Then you will revise and edit your report. The last step is to publish it.

You may want to use pictures or graphs in your paper. These help break up the text. They are also another way to give information to the reader.

Photographs and captions help make the subject clearer.

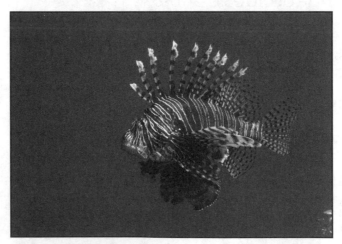

A lionfish's spines look like feathers.

© The Continental Press, Inc.   DUPLICATING THIS MATERIAL IS ILLEGAL.

Charts, tables, diagrams, and maps show examples that help you understand what you are reading.

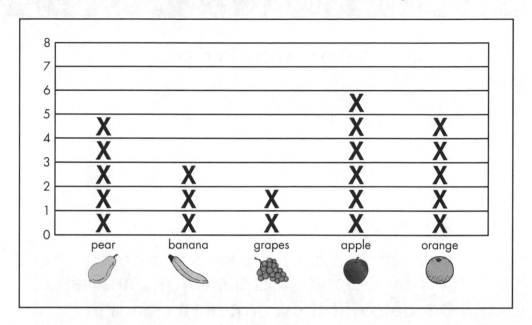

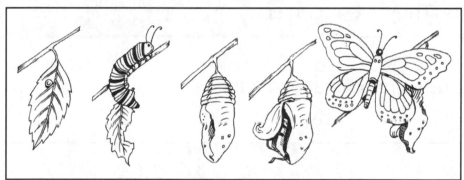

A butterfly changes as it grows.

MISSISSIPPI RIVER DELTA

© The Continental Press, Inc.   DUPLICATING THIS MATERIAL IS ILLEGAL.

Guided Practice

Which of these would be helpful to show where Florida is in the United States?

A map

B photograph

C diagram

D chart

 A map is the best choice. Choice A is the correct answer. Choices B, C, and D would not show where Florida is in the United States. They are incorrect.

Explain why you would use a photograph in a report.

_____

_____

_____

 Think about what you can learn from a photograph. Does it help you compare two things? Does it show where something is located? Here is a sample answer:

A photograph would be helpful in a report to show what something looks like. You could use a photograph of a whale to show what it looks like.

© The Continental Press, Inc.   DUPLICATING THIS MATERIAL IS ILLEGAL.

Step 6: Tell the Sources

An important part of the research paper is telling where you found your facts. This helps readers know what sources you used.

Readers want to know
- where you found your facts (title)
- who created it (the author and the publisher)
- when they created it (year)

Most reports will have two or more sources. You make a list of these sources for a report. This is a called a **bibliography.** This list goes at the end of your paper.

Here is how to list a book:

Author's last name, author's first name. Title. City where published: name of publisher, date published.

Here is how to list a website:

"Title." Website address. Date you found information.

This is an example of a bibliography.

Bibliography

Davis, Henry. Seahorses. New York: Science Book Press, 2011.

"Seahorses." http://www.aqua.org. March 15, 2011.

"Seahorses." http://www.nationalgeographic.com. March 15, 2011.

Tellez, Antonio. Tiny Seahorses. New York: Ocean Press, 2011.

© The Continental Press, Inc.   DUPLICATING THIS MATERIAL IS ILLEGAL.

Guided Practice

Read the questions. Then answer them.

Which is the correct listing for a website?

A "Sharks." www.nationalaquarium.org. April 2, 2011.

B April 2, 2011. "Sharks." www.nationalaquarium.org.

C www.nationalaquarium.org. "Sharks." April 2, 2011.

D "Sharks." April 2, 2011. www.nationalaquarium.org

 Choice A is the correct answer. It lists the title first. Then it lists the place where the facts were found. The date the website was visited is also listed. Choices B, C, and D are incorrect.

Kaeden used a book called <u>Beneath the Sea</u>. The author was Kasey Reynolds. The book was published in 2010. The publisher was Ocean Press. They are in New York City. Write a source listing using this information.

_____

_____

 The information goes in a certain order. Who, what, where, and when is the order. Here is a sample answer:

Reynolds, Kasey. <u>Beneath the Sea</u>. New York: Ocean Press, 2010.

Publishing the Paper

You can publish your paper many ways. You can use a computer to write it and then give your teacher a copy. Another way to publish your report is to make a poster using the facts in the report.

174
UNIT 3
Research

© The Continental Press, Inc.   DUPLICATING THIS MATERIAL IS ILLEGAL.

Test Yourself

1 Why should you list your sources?

_____

_____

_____

_____

2 Where would you find a source list, or bibliography?

_____

_____

_____

_____

© The Continental Press, Inc.　DUPLICATING THIS MATERIAL IS ILLEGAL.

3 List three different types of visual aids you could use in a report about seahorses.

_____

_____

_____

_____

_____

4 Which would you <u>most likely</u> find in a report about an author?

   A a map showing where the author lives

   B a photograph of the author

   C a table telling how long it took the author to write each book

   D a graph showing how many books the author sold

5 Which is the correct listing for a book in a source list?

   A <u>My Favorite Sea Creatures</u>. Dr. Frank James. 2011, Ocean Press.

   B James, Dr. Frank. <u>My Favorite Sea Creatures</u>. New York: Ocean Press, 2011.

   C New York: Ocean Press, 2011. Dr. Frank James. <u>My Favorite Sea Creatures</u>.

   D <u>My Favorite Sea Creatures</u>. 2011, New York: Ocean Press. Dr. Frank James.

© The Continental Press, Inc. DUPLICATING THIS MATERIAL IS ILLEGAL.

Language Conventions

Good writing starts with good sentences. This unit looks at the rules that help you write clear sentences.

- **Lesson 13** covers punctuation and capitalization rules.

- **In Lesson 14,** you will review the grammar rules you have learned. These rules help you to write clear sentences.

© The Continental Press, Inc.   DUPLICATING THIS MATERIAL IS ILLEGAL.

Language Conventions

W.2.5; L.2.1, 2

Good writers know what punctuation to use. They also use proper capitalization and spelling.

Capitalization

Begin every sentence with a capital letter.

Incorrect   the cab driver honked the horn.

Correct   The cab driver honked the horn.

Begin words that name people, places, holidays, days of the week, and months with capital letters.

People	Places	Days, Months, Things
Jim Bowie	Niagara Falls	Monday
Clara Barton	Charleston, South Carolina	February
Luis Nuncio	Lake Erie	Kleenex tissues

Guided Practice

Underline the words in each sentence that need a capital letter.

we took a walk down maple street.

Dara's family stays at malibu beach every july.

 The name of a person, place, day of the week, or month is capitalized. Here are the correct answers:

<u>we</u> took a walk down <u>maple</u> <u>street</u>.

Dara's family stays at <u>malibu</u> <u>beach</u> every <u>july</u>.

© The Continental Press, Inc. DUPLICATING THIS MATERIAL IS ILLEGAL.

Punctuation

A sentence that makes a statement ends with a **period.**

Statement   Bats eat insects.

A sentence that gives a command, or tells you what to do, also ends with a **period.**

Command   Wait for me, please.

A sentence that asks a question ends with a **question mark.**

Question   Did you go to the school play?

Questions often begin with the following words: who, what, when, where, why, and how. Sometimes, they begin with a verb.

Is Julio walking to school?

A sentence that expresses a strong feeling ends with an **exclamation mark.**

Exclamation   That was an exciting game!

A **comma** is used after a greeting or closing in a letter.

Greeting   Dear Jovanna,
Closing   Sincerely,

© The Continental Press, Inc.   DUPLICATING THIS MATERIAL IS ILLEGAL.

Guided Practice

Add the correct punctuation to the items below.

Sam waited an hour for his dad

Where was Dad

There he is

Dear Kevin

 Punctuation marks help the reader know what is being said. Here are the correct answers:

Sam waited an hour for his dad.

Where was Dad?

There he is!

Dear Kevin,

Apostrophe

Use an **apostrophe** to form a contraction. A **contraction** is the short form of two words. The apostrophe takes the place of the missing letter or letters.

are not	aren't	is not	isn't
I am	I'm	it is	it's
they will	they'll	you will	you'll

Think about the two words that form a contraction. That will help you write the correct word.

| **Incorrect** | Its Thursday. |
| **Correct** | It's Thursday. |

| **Incorrect** | There good friends. |
| **Correct** | They're good friends |

© The Continental Press, Inc.   DUPLICATING THIS MATERIAL IS ILLEGAL.

Use an apostrophe and –s to show ownership, or possession. If a noun is singular, add an apostrophe and –s to make it possessive. A singular noun that ends in s still has an apostrophe and an –s added.

Michael's baseball cap is on the chair.

Mrs. **Jones's** grew tomatoes in her garden.

If a noun is plural, add just an apostrophe to make it possessive.

The **girls'** awards were on display.

Guided Practice

Write the contraction for the underlined words.

I see that <u>you are</u> ready to work. _____

We can go outside if <u>it is</u> not raining. _____

Mom and Dad said <u>they will</u> call. _____

✔ Contractions are two words that have been joined. The letters that are missing are noted with an apostrophe. Here are the correct answers:

I see that <u>you are</u> ready to work. _____you're_____

We can go outside if <u>it is</u> not raining. _____it's_____

Mom and Dad said <u>they will</u> call. _____they'll_____

© The Continental Press, Inc.   DUPLICATING THIS MATERIAL IS ILLEGAL.

In each sentence, write the possessive form of the noun in parentheses on the line.

The _____ meowing is loud. (cats)

Mr. _____ hat blew off. (James)

✓ You form the possessive with an apostrophe and an –s. Here are the correct answers:

The _____cat's_____ meowing is loud.

Mr. _____James's_____ hat blew off.

© The Continental Press, Inc.   DUPLICATING THIS MATERIAL IS ILLEGAL.

Test Yourself

Write the contraction for the underlined words.

1 <u>We are</u> so pleased to meet you. _____

2 Olivia said that <u>she is</u> on the bus. _____

Edit this paragraph.

3

i want to bake a cake for mom's birthday.
what do you think I should make should it
be chocolate or vanilla i think she likes
both. maybe dad could help me bake the cake
i could make chocolate frosting. mom will
be so surprised

© The Continental Press, Inc. DUPLICATING THIS MATERIAL IS ILLEGAL.

Grammar

W.2.5; L.2.1, 2

We use sentences when we write. A **sentence** is a group of words that tells a whole, or complete, thought.

Subject and Verb

Every sentence has two parts: a **subject** and a **verb.**

The subject tells who or what is doing the action in a sentence. The subject is usually the first part of a sentence. A subject is often a **noun.** It can also be a pronoun. A pronoun takes the place of a noun.

The **verb** tells something about the subject. It shows what the subject does. The verb is usually the second part of the sentence.

The kitten chased the ball of yarn.

The subject in the sentence is kitten.
The verb is chased.

Guided Practice

In each sentence, circle the subject and underline the verb.

Kenesha swung the jump rope.

The dog chewed my shoe.

 The subject is what does the action. The verb shows action. Here are the correct answers:

(Kenesha) swung the jump rope.

The (dog) chewed my shoe.

© The Continental Press, Inc. DUPLICATING THIS MATERIAL IS ILLEGAL.

Singular and Plural Nouns

A **singular noun** is one person, place, or thing. A **plural noun** is more than one person, place, or thing. Usually, plural nouns end in -s.

Singular Noun	Plural Noun
boy	boys
field	fields
dog	dogs

There are some plural nouns that do not end in -s. These are called **irregular plural nouns.** Here are some examples of irregular plural nouns.

Singular Noun	Plural Noun
child	children
mouse	mice
foot	feet
goose	geese

Guided Practice

Decide whether each noun is singular or plural. Next, to each word write an S for singular or a P for plural.

ox _____

women _____

tooth _____

✓ Singular is one. Plural is more than one. Here are the correct answers:

ox _____S_____

women _____P_____

tooth _____S_____

© The Continental Press, Inc.   DUPLICATING THIS MATERIAL IS ILLEGAL.

Collective Nouns

These nouns tell about many that belong to one group. These nouns take a singular verb.

Incorrect	The group are going to the movies.
Correct	The group is going to the movies.
Incorrect	That team are the winner.
Correct	That team is the winner.

Guided Practice

Write the correct verb on the line.

The school board (is, are) about to vote. _____

The jury (vote, votes) on the case in an hour. _____

 Collective nouns are singular. They take a singular verb. Here are the correct answers:

The school board (is, are) about to vote. _____is_____

The jury (vote, votes) on the case in an hour. _____votes_____

Pronouns

Pronouns take the place of nouns. The –self pronouns are used to tell about people or things doing something on their own. Here is a list of these pronouns:

Singular	myself	yourself	himself	herself	itself
Plural	ourselves	yourselves	themselves		

Adele bought **herself** new skates.
Joe and Jack bought **themselves** new shoes.

© The Continental Press, Inc. DUPLICATING THIS MATERIAL IS ILLEGAL.

Guided Practice

The bird built _____ a nest.

Kim and Kelly are going to get _____
into trouble.

> Think about what pronoun takes the place of the noun.
> Then add –self. Here are the correct answers:

The bird built _____itself_____ a nest.

Kim and Kelly are going to get _themselves_
into trouble.

Verbs

A verb in the **present tense** tells what is happening
now or what keeps on happening. A verb in the **past
tense** tells what happened before, or in the past.

Read each pair of sentences below. The verbs are
underlined. Notice the ending –ed is added to each past-tense
verb. Most verbs form the past tense with –ed.

Present Tense	Fresh bread smells great.
Past Tense	Yesterday, the bread smelled great.
Present Tense	Bees hum in the garden.
Past Tense	Bees hummed in the garden.

© The Continental Press, Inc.   DUPLICATING THIS MATERIAL IS ILLEGAL.

Forms of Be

The verb be is **irregular.** It changes to a different word for the past tense. The form of the verb must also match the subject. This chart shows when to use different forms of the verb be.

Subject	Present Tense	Past Tense
Singular Pronouns		
I	am	was
you	are	were
he, she, it	is	was
Plural Pronouns		
we	are	were
they	are	were
Singular Nouns	is	was
Plural Nouns	are	were

Irregular Verbs

The past tense of most verbs is formed by adding –ed. Some verbs have a different spelling and sound in the past tense. This chart shows some irregular verbs that are often used.

Irregular Verbs	
Present Tense	**Past Tense**
eat	ate
fly	flew
give	gave
hide	hid
know	knew
say	said
sit	sat
take	took
tell	told

© The Continental Press, Inc.   DUPLICATING THIS MATERIAL IS ILLEGAL.

Guided Practice

Underline the verb in each sentence. Then write whether it is in present tense or past tense.

Darell flew the plane over our house. _____

A cat sat in the window. _____

My dad likes cream in his coffee. _____

✓ Past tense means it already took place. Present tense means it is happening now. Here are the correct answers:

Darell <u>flew</u> the plane over our house. _____*past*_____

A cat <u>sat</u> in the window. _____*past*_____

My dad <u>likes</u> cream in his coffee. _____*present*_____

Choose the correct form of the verb <u>be</u>. Write it on the line.

My name _____ Adam. (is, am)

They _____ here last night. (was, were)

✓ The verb must match the subject. Here are the correct answers:

My name _____*is*_____ Adam. (is, am)

They _____*were*_____ here last night. (was, were)

© The Continental Press, Inc. DUPLICATING THIS MATERIAL IS ILLEGAL.

Adjectives and Adverbs

An **adjective** is a word that describes a person, an animal, a place, or a thing.

An adjective may answer the question: What kind?
> A **red** car drove by. (what kind of car?)

An adjective may answer the questions: How many? How much?
> **Three** plants grew. (how many plants?)

An adjective may come after the noun or pronoun it describes.
> I am **happy.** (describes I)
> The houses are **old.** (describes houses)

Two or more adjectives may come before or after the word they describe. You may need to use commas to separate the adjectives.
> The flag is **red, white,** and **blue.**

Choose adjectives with care. Use an adjective that makes a clear, specific picture of what you mean.

Not Specific	The dog is **nice.**
Specific	The dog is **cuddly.**
Not Specific	We had a **bad** week.
Specific	We had a **stormy** week.

© The Continental Press, Inc.   DUPLICATING THIS MATERIAL IS ILLEGAL.

Guided Practice

Cross out the adjective that is not specific. Write a better one on the line.

great story   _____

nice house   _____

bad day   _____

The adjectives do not help you picture the house or the day. You need to use an adjective that helps the reader see the house. Here are sample answers:

~~great~~ story   _____scary_____

~~nice~~ house   _____yellow_____

~~bad~~ day   _____rainy_____

Adverbs

Words called **adverbs** tell how actions are done. The adverb in each sentence is in bold type.

> Emily planned **carefully.** (tells how she planned)
> She painted **slowly.** (tells how she painted)

The words <u>carefully</u> and <u>slowly</u> have the same ending, or suffix. Each adverb is made from an adjective and the suffix –<u>ly</u>.

> careful + -ly   =   carefully
> slow + -ly   =   slowly

© The Continental Press, Inc.   DUPLICATING THIS MATERIAL IS ILLEGAL.

Many adverbs are made by adding –ly to an adjective.

The man had a **loud** voice. He spoke **loudly.**
(Loud is an adjective. Loudly is an adverb.)

Remember to use the word with the suffix –ly when you tell how an action is done.

Incorrect   A bird sang sweet. It hopped quick.
Correct   A bird sang sweetly. It hopped quickly.

Guided Practice

Add –ly to each word to turn it into an adverb.

sad _____

soft _____

> ✓ You form an adverb from an adjective. You do this by adding –ly. Here are the correct answers:

sad _____ _sadly_____

soft _____ _softly_____

Cross out the incorrect word in the sentence. Write the correct word on the line.

The crowd shouted noisy. _____

The dancer pointed her toe graceful. _____

> ✓ An adverb tells how actions are done. An adjective describes how something is. Here are the correct answers:

The crowd shouted ~~noisy~~. _____ _noisily_____

The dancer pointed her toe ~~graceful~~. _____ _gracefully_____

192 UNIT 4 ▓▓
Language Conventions

© The Continental Press, Inc.   DUPLICATING THIS MATERIAL IS ILLEGAL.

Test Yourself

Read the story. Find and fix any mistakes. Cross out each mistake, and write the correction above it.

1   The Lion and the Mouse

Long, long ago, a lion were in his den. Him

was fast asleep. A mouse come in and jumped on

the lion's nose. The lion be angry! He grab the

mouse by the tail.

"Please don't hurt me," say the mouse. "Me and

you should be friends. One day youl need my help."

The lion just laugh. "A big lion need no help

from a little mouse," he said. "But Ile let you

go anyway." He put her down, and they ran away.

A few days later, the lion step into a huge

net. It trapped him. "My feet is stuck!" the lion

roared. "Them can't move!"

© The Continental Press, Inc.   DUPLICATING THIS MATERIAL IS ILLEGAL.

The mouse heard the roars. She knowed the lion

was in trouble, so she raced to him. Then she

use her teeth. She chewed right through the net.

The lion and her ran to safety.

The lion said to the mouse, "You were right. A

mouse help a lion sometimes. Your a good friend."

Cross out the incorrect word in the sentence. Write the correct word on the line.

2 The cat stretched lazy on the couch. _____

3 The boy ran quick down the field. _____

Write a -self pronoun on the line.

4 She bought _____ an ice cream cone.

5 They drove _____ here.

Complete each sentence. Write an adverb on the line.

6 "Thank you for the gift!" said Mom _____.

7 Snow fell _____ on the ground.

© The Continental Press, Inc.   DUPLICATING THIS MATERIAL IS ILLEGAL.

PRACTICE TEST

It's Early to Rise for the Local Baker!

Have you ever thought about how your bread is made? Did you ever try to make a cake or cookies yourself? Your local baker thinks about these things all the time. It's all part of the job!

A baker has to be up early in the morning. This is to make sure that the bakery shelves are full by the time customers arrive. In a small bakery, everything is made by hand. It takes a lot of work to make cakes, cookies, pies, and bread.

The baker has to be good at math. Every ingredient in a recipe has to be measured. The baker also has to know how to use kitchen tools like a mixer, measuring cups and spoons, and most important of all, the oven. Kitchen safety is very important in a bakery. Bakers know how to use the right tools in a safe way.

A baker also has to have a good imagination and a large collection of recipes. A good baker will always try to come up with a new treat for customers. Many bakers make up their own recipes!

© The Continental Press, Inc. DUPLICATING THIS MATERIAL IS ILLEGAL.

Every baker starts off as a beginner. Most bakers have favorite recipes handed down to them by the person who taught them to bake. Sometimes, they learn from their families or from another baker in a shop. Sometimes, they go to cooking school to learn how to bake. Bakers learn to use recipes that they know will work well. It's important for a baker to follow instructions on recipes. That way, the final product is sure to be delicious!

1 What are three important qualities a baker must have?

_____

_____

_____

_____

© The Continental Press, Inc.   DUPLICATING THIS MATERIAL IS ILLEGAL.

2 What are two ways that someone might learn to bake?

_____

_____

_____

_____

_____

3 Read the question. Then plan, write, revise, and edit your answer.

> Pretend that your mother runs a bakery, and your family lives upstairs. On Saturday mornings, you go downstairs at 6 a.m. to help your mother. It is your job to put the rolls and cookies on trays in a glass case. Write a story about doing your job one day. In your story, be sure to include:
>
> • a topic sentence about your job
>
> • a beginning, middle, and end to your story
>
> • details to make the story interesting

© The Continental Press, Inc.   DUPLICATING THIS MATERIAL IS ILLEGAL.

Prewriting

Underline or mark up the question as you wish. Then use this page to plan your answer. Choose a graphic organizer to plan your answer.

_____

_____

_____

_____

_____

_____

_____

_____

_____

_____

_____

_____

© The Continental Press, Inc.   DUPLICATING THIS MATERIAL IS ILLEGAL.

Drafting

Use this page to write your draft.

_____

_____

_____

_____

_____

_____

_____

_____

_____

_____

_____

_____

_____

_____

© The Continental Press, Inc.   DUPLICATING THIS MATERIAL IS ILLEGAL.

Revising and Editing

Use this page to revise your draft. Then edit your work.

_____

_____

_____

_____

_____

_____

_____

_____

_____

_____

_____

_____

_____

Practice Test

© The Continental Press, Inc.   DUPLICATING THIS MATERIAL IS ILLEGAL.

Publishing

Write your final copy on the page below. Then show it to your teacher.

_____

_____

_____

_____

_____

_____

_____

_____

_____

_____

_____

_____

_____

▓▓▓▓ Publishing ▓▓▓▓▓▓▓▓▓▓▓▓▓▓▓▓▓▓▓▓▓▓▓▓▓▓▓▓▓▓▓▓▓▓▓▓▓

© The Continental Press, Inc.   DUPLICATING THIS MATERIAL IS ILLEGAL.

Edit this paper for mistakes. Write your corrections on the essay. Be sure to use the proofreading marks you know.

My uncle Chet runs bakery in Levittown. He always love to cook. He learned to bake from his mother my grandmother. He learnd when he was only 6 years old. He helped his mother in the kitchen all the time. She taut him to measure ingredients and use the mixer. He made up his first cake recipe when he was 8!

Uncle Chet can cook anything real well. his favorite thing to make is bagels. Everybody loves Uncle Chets bagels. People line up every morning at the bakery to get them erly. If you get to Uncle Chet's bakery too late all the bagels are gone!

Practice Test

© The Continental Press, Inc.   DUPLICATING THIS MATERIAL IS ILLEGAL.

HANDBOOK

Using Capital Letters

- Begin every sentence with a capital letter: **M**y bike is green.

- Begin each part of a person's name with a capital letter. Include titles that are used as part of the name.

    Ryan **W. C**ooper   **A**unt **R**osa

    President **A**dams   **D**r. **C**hen

- Begin words that name days, months, holidays, and places with a capital letter.

    Monday   **O**ctober   **F**lag **D**ay

    Riverside **S**chool   **N**ew **Y**ork **C**ity

- Do NOT begin the names of seasons with a capital letter.

    winter   fall   spring   summer

Using Punctuation Marks
End Marks

- End every sentence with a period (**.**), a question mark (**?**), or an exclamation point (**!**).

- End a statement with a period: Tadpoles turn into frogs**.**

- End a question with a question mark: Where is your jacket**?**

- End an exclamation with an exclamation point: I love summer**!**

© The Continental Press, Inc.   DUPLICATING THIS MATERIAL IS ILLEGAL.

Commas (,)

- When two sentences are joined by <u>and</u>, <u>but</u>, or <u>or</u>, use a comma before the joining word.

    Tyler played checkers, **and** Elizabeth read a book.

- Use commas between words that name things in a group.

    Mix together the flour, sugar, salt, and oil.

- Use a comma between the day and year in a date.

    April 7, 2011

- Use a comma between a city and state.

    Omaha, Nebraska

Apostrophes (')

- Use an apostrophe to show who owns or has something. If the owner is singular (one person or thing), add an apostrophe and <u>-s</u>.

    Matt**'s** dad   a duck**'s** beak

- If the owner is plural (more than one) and ends in <u>-s</u>, add just an apostrophe.

    three girl**s'** scores   all the cat**s'** tails

- Use an apostrophe to show where letters are missing in a contraction.

    I + am = I'm (<u>a</u> is missing)
    is + not = isn't (<u>o</u> is missing)

Quotation Marks (" ")

- Use quotation marks before and after the words a person says.

    Jessica said, "I will play my violin."

© The Continental Press, Inc.   DUPLICATING THIS MATERIAL IS ILLEGAL.

Using Correct Grammar

Subject-Verb Agreement

- When you use an action verb in the present tense, add -s or -es to the verb if the subject is a singular noun (one person or thing). Do not add -s or -es to the verb if the subject is plural (more than one).

  > Emily sing**s**   children sing   Carlos and Becky sing

- If the subject is a pronoun, add -s or -es to the verb only if the pronoun is he, she, or it.

  > he eat**s**   I eat   you eat   we eat   they eat

Subject-Verb Agreement with Forms of *be*

- If the subject is a singular noun (one person or thing), use is for the present tense and was for the past tense.

  > Kayla **is**   the sky **was**

- If the subject is a plural noun or more than one noun, use are for the present tense and were for the past tense.

  > Wrong: the pencils **is**   Wrong: the pen and pencil **was**

  > Correct: the pencils **are**   Correct: the pen and pencil **were**

- Use the correct form of be with a singular or plural pronoun subject.

Present Tense		Past Tense	
Singular	Plural	Singular	Plural
I **am**	we **are**	I **was**	we **were**
you **are**	you **are**	you **were**	you **were**
he, she, or it **is**	they **are**	he, she, or it **was**	they **were**

© The Continental Press, Inc.   DUPLICATING THIS MATERIAL IS ILLEGAL.

Irregular Verbs

Many past tense verbs do not end in -ed. It will help to learn the correct forms by heart.

Present	Past	Past Participle
is	was	(has) been
begin	began	(has) begun
bring	brought	(has) brought
choose	chose	(has) chosen
come	came	(has) come
go	went	(has) gone
have	had	(has) had
know	knew	(has) known
make	made	(has) made
run	ran	(has) run
say	said	(has) said
take	took	(has) taken
write	wrote	(has) written

© The Continental Press, Inc.   DUPLICATING THIS MATERIAL IS ILLEGAL.

Proofreading Symbols

∧	Add letters or words.	He had a ^{mountain} bike.
⊙	Add a period.	I liked mountain bikes, too⊙
≡	Capitalize a letter.	i̳t was small.
⋏	Add a comma.	When I was 5⋏ I wanted to ride a bike.
⨍	Delete letters or words.	My dad h̶e̶ said he would teach me.
∿	Switch the position of letters or words.	I learned finally how to ride a bike.

© The Continental Press, Inc.   DUPLICATING THIS MATERIAL IS ILLEGAL.

Notes